My Invented Land

My Invented Land

NEW AND SELECTED POEMS

Robin S. Ngangom

SPEAKING
TIGER

SPEAKING TIGER BOOKS LLP
125A, Ground Floor, Shahpur Jat, near Asiad Village,
New Delhi 110049

First published by Speaking Tiger Books 2023

ISBN: 978-93-5447-401-9
eISBN: 978-93-5447-405-7

10 9 8 7 6 5 4 3 2 1

Typeset in ArnhemFine Normal by SÜRYA, New Delhi

Printed at ...

For Sumita, Changning, and Chingleí
Mālém, nūmit, thā

CONTENTS

THE DESIRE OF ROOTS (2006)

INTRODUCTION

I wrote my first faltering line in the relative innocence of childhood. I was about eleven or twelve years old then, and caught as I was in the flush of youth, I wanted to explore the world by writing ornate and sentimental poetry. Since life was ignoring me, I thought I could engage the attention of kindred hearts through friendly and soft-hearted verse. Naturally, my poems were mostly inspired by romances and adventure stories, especially *The Thousand and One Nights*, but it was essentially dreamy-eyed adolescent stuff. I still haven't grown out of it.

One favourite poem of mine began with the line: 'The boy stood on the burning deck'. That well-meaning world is no longer recognisable now; the sacred landmarks have disappeared long since. Only dim memories of hoisting the country's flag on a holiday, or leading a blind man by the hand, or praying in temples on a feast day, remain as mute reminders of that sacred past.

Manipur, my native place in Northeast India, is in a state of anarchy, and my poetry springs from the cruel contradictions of that land. Manipur boasts of its talents in theatre, cinema, dance and sports. But how could you trust your own people when they entrust corruption, AIDS, terrorism and drugs to their children? Naturally, the Manipur that I ritually go back to from the laid-back hill town of Shillong every year is not the sacred world of my childhood, because:

Childhood took place
free from manly fears
when I had only my mother's love
to protect me from knives,
from fire, and death by water.
I wore it like an amulet.
Childhood took place
among fairies and weretigers
when hills were yours to tumble
before they became soldiers' barracks
and dreaded chambers of torture.
Childhood took place
before your friend worshipped a gun
to become a widowmaker.

Having acknowledged this growing restlessness within myself, poetry
became an outlet for pent-up feelings and desires, where I can bare
myself without actually being demonstrative. Poetry, therefore, has
remained an underground exercise with me. It perhaps began as a
dialogue with the self, and has become an illegitimate affair of the
heart, because I believe in the poetry of 'feeling', which can be shared;
not cerebral, intellectual poetry which is inaccessible, and which
leaves the reader outside the poet's insulated world. I suppose I've
always tried in a naive way to invite the reader into my small world.
Perhaps I've written poems because I've felt this desperate need to
be understood, and to be accepted:

I want to describe myself again and again
to people who do not know me.
That is why I always look for paper and ink,
even in the midst of a terrible loss,
or, a dangerous illness.
Because someone said

the spoken word flies
but the written word stays.

In many ways, my own Meitei culture, which is part of my childhood, has shaped my thinking. Perhaps we all mourn the fate of our homeland, as the Sicilian poet Quasimodo has said. And though I've never remotely imagined myself as any conscience-keeper, I've often tried to speak of my people, and of the terrible things happening in Manipur:

First came the scream of the dying
in a bad dream, then the radio report,
and a newspaper: six shot dead, twenty-five
houses razed, sixteen beheaded with hands tied
behind their backs inside a church.
As the days crumbled, and the victors
and their victims grew in number,
I hardened inside my thickening hide,
until I lost my tenuous humanity.
I ceased thinking
of abandoned children inside blazing huts
still waiting for their parents.
If they remembered their grandmothers' tales
of many winter hearths at the hour
of sleeping death, I didn't want to know,
if they ever learnt the magic of letters.
And the women heavy with seed,
their soft bodies mown down
like grain stalk during their lyric harvests;
if they wore wildflowers in their hair
while they waited for their men,
I didn't care anymore.
I burnt my truth with them,

And buried uneasy manhood with them.
I did mutter, on some far-off day:
'There are limits,' but when the day
absolved the butchers, I continued to live
as if nothing happened.

I don't agree with the view that a writer requires a tradition to lean upon, to till the soil which others have made fertile, and harvest ideas for himself. A writer can be influenced by anything, and he would be able to write in any country other than his own. But he has to reclaim his individual voice. It is natural for someone from the Northeast of India to exploit the folk traditions he grew up with, to write of the hills when he is living in the hills. It is Shillong that has moved me into this kind of poetry, Shillong with its gentle hills, the Khasis with their rich oral literature:

I told you the stories of old
on soft Sundays, of Manik Raitong
and Ka Likai. Only the stones of unknown gorges
weep for them, I said.
We awakened sleeping melodies
and talked of native lands,
and my foolish youth.
Where the pines
read the lips of the wind
and silent rain drums the hills,
the cottages dry their eyes
and open them in the dusk.
The land of the seven huts,
they've named these hills.
You would belong here
if you would listen to your heart.

If I had not made use of this hillworld, my poetry would have been false. You would notice this preponderance of images from the hills in many of my poems—the vast pines, the mountains with their great rains. But this, I've realised, is mostly artless, inoffensive poetry. For someone who has suffered from a fundamental poverty of experience, I've been naturally inclined towards the personal lyric. I don't have faith in inspiration, but since poetry cannot originate in a vacuum, I've also left my influences open, and have allowed myself to be ambushed by political events, books, biased memory, a dogged sexuality, womankind, films, streets even.

But my poetry seems to be drifting towards something 'more'. It is no longer a mere diary of private incidents, or a confessional. I've been trying to come to terms with this change of heart, which is even more distressing than the shattered love of a woman. And I've perhaps opened my eyes to insistent realities and have stepped out of the proverbial ivory tower. If anyone should ask now why my poems do not speak of my land's breathtaking landscapes, its sinuous dances, its dark-maned women, I can only offer Neruda's answer: 'Come and see the blood in the streets!'

The writer from Northeast India, consequently, differs from his counterpart in the mainland in a significant way. While it may not make him a better writer, living with the menace of the gun does not permit him to indulge in verbal wizardry or woolly aesthetics, but is a constant reminder that he must perforce master 'the art of witness' (Michael Ignatieff. 'The Art of Witness', *The New York Review of Books*, Vol. XLII, No. 5, 23 March 1995). Forces working under slogans that have been twisted, slogans such as 'self-determination', rive my society. We have witnessed growing ethnic aggressiveness, secessionist ventures, cultural and religious bigotry, the marginalisation of minorities and the poor, profit and power struggles in government, and as a natural aftermath to these, the banality of corruption and the banality of terror.

Further, the uneasy coexistence of paradoxical worlds such as the folk and the Westernised, virgin forests and car-choked streets, ethnic cleansers and the parasites of democracy, ancestral values and flagrant materialism, resurgent nativism and the sensitive outsider's predicament, make the picturesque Northeast especially vulnerable to tragedy. And what can a poet-aspirant do in such contrary circumstances, when he can no longer nurse a magical vision of the world?

For the first time, I've begun to understand Camus's words: 'Whatever our personal weaknesses may be, the nobility of our craft will always be rooted in two commitments, difficult to maintain: the refusal to lie about what one knows and the resistance to oppression' (Nobel Prize acceptance speech, 1957). Today, when cruel suppositions are made about the conceit of the artist, innuendoes that the poet has become a world unto himself and should be brought to his knees; when there is a sharp divide between modish criticism and literature, when literary schools are merely reactionary and seem to be turning their eyes from what is known as the human condition, I would again like to reaffirm my indebtedness to my fellow men.

Today, when heartrending events are happening all around a poet, when all he hears are chilling accounts of what man has done to man, how can he close his eyes to the brutalisation of life and remain solipsistic? Anyone with even an iota of conviction is in immediate danger if he speaks up; a gun points at you if you don't observe a prescribed code of behaviour—how then can I claim that I am living in a free society?

In contemporary Manipuri poetry, there is a predominance of images of bullets, blood, mother, the colour red and, paradoxically, flowers too. A poet from Imphal told me how they've been honing 'the poetry of survival' with guns pressed to both temples: the gun of revolution and the gun of the state. Hardly anyone writes romantic verse or talks about disturbing aspects of sexuality because they are absorbed in writing the poetry of survival. This has resulted in criticism that contemporary Manipuri poetry is hemmed in by extreme realism.

There is, of course, a danger of the images listed above becoming hackneyed. And maybe poets should try to strike that fine balance between realism and reflection, as Israeli poet Yehuda Amichai skilfully does in 'The Diameter of the Bomb'. The opening lines of this poem read like statistics and a news report that we often ignore as we go on with our daily lives: 'The diameter of the bomb was thirty centimetres/and the diameter of its effective range about seven metres,/with four dead and eleven wounded.' But the lines that follow make us reflect on lives obliterated by violence; they reveal how violence transforms men and women, regardless of nationalities; and also how such mindless acts make one reflect on the indifference of a god who, if he exists at all, should never have allowed his creation to be erased or reduced to an absurd drama.

But poets also have to write about the here and now. And writing about it lends a sense of immediacy and vividness to their poetry. I call this the 'poetry of witness'.

In Manipur, when the reality becomes oppressive, a few poets frequently seek refuge in absurdist irony often directed towards oneself, in parody, and in satire. It is a rejection by these poets of the extreme realism I've mentioned; they in turn, also reveal an inclination towards the surreal. In Manipuri poet Y. Ibomcha's 'Story of a Dream', murderous bullets turn into luscious fruits, and in Thangjam Ibopishak's 'I Want to be Killed by an Indian Bullet', terrorists appear in the guise of the five elements. This kind of verse is a reaction to the absurdity of violence and death, when the Manipuri poet's existence is reduced to negotiating the subject matter of guiltless addicts, child soldiers and young mothers with AIDS.

Literature that is not the breath of contemporary society, that dares not transmit the pains and fears of that society, that does not warn in time against threatening moral and social dangers—such literature does not deserve the name of literature; it is only a facade, claims Alexander Solzhenitsyn. But here lies a paradox, because the writer is not beholden to anyone, let alone to society. He must be true only to his own world and to himself. A writer is not a self-assigned conscience-keeper. Living in society, he will talk about his milieu, the people with whom he is in touch with daily. But you cannot expect a writer to consciously promote, say, ethnic harmony, as a part of his writing programme. You cannot expect a writer to be a public relations official on behalf of any organisation, or a propagandist for any cause. On the other hand, there is often a defiant and self-damaging streak in him that sometimes incites him to confront authority.

In 1964, when Joseph Brodsky was asked by Soviet authorities what he did for a living and he replied that he wrote poetry; he was immediately arrested on the charge of 'social parasitism'. Is the writer a 'social parasite' or a 'conscience-keeper' for his society? One thing is certain: he values his freedom above everything else, and will protect it fiercely. I think the task that literature of the Northeast must address is what Albert Camus called 'the double challenge of truth and liberty'. Truth, because what can the writer hope to accomplish now except to tell the truth?

When the unspeakable is out there, being enacted and quickly consigned to oblivion, when cruel things are done but never undone, and when media machines are busy feeding the world one-sided lies, the writer can only tell the truth about what he knows. Literature cannot bring harmony or a moral revolution by telling us what we must do. And forces are always at work to rob the writer of his freedom. Liberty, therefore, is a necessary precondition, which the writer must fight for in order to tell the truth he knows; freedom is the lifeblood of his art.

During these pessimistic times, the responsibility of the writer is much more modest than what well-meaning people would like him to shoulder, that is, to change the world into a better place through his efforts. But at most, poetry of the Northeast can only mirror the body and the mind of the times, as in Thangjam Ibopishak's 'Poem':

> Now, in this country
> One cannot speak aloud,
> One cannot think in the open.
> Hence 'poem',
> Like a flower I sport with you.
> Before my eyes, incident upon incident,
> Awesome, heaving events,
> Walking, yet sleeping,
> Eyes open, but dreaming,
> Standing, yet having nightmares;
> In dreams, and in reality
> Only fearsome, shivery instances.
> So around me, closing eyes,
> Palms on ears,
> Moulding the heart to a mere clay object,
> I write poems about flowers.
> Now, in this land
> One should only think of flowers,
> Dream about flowers,
> For my little baby, my wife,
> For my job,
> To protect myself from harm.

Surrounded as we are by playthings we don't need, when a man's worth is determined by what he can buy, we are continuously taught to be grateful to the capitalist god. What we have inherited then are the tyrannical fetishes of market capitalism, murderous technologies and grisly ideologies that would leave a cursed earth for our children. How can poetry sing the praises of this age, or compose hymns to Mammon? For me, poetry can never be an ally of this numbing materialism or a party to mindless violence. Materialism, wherever it abounds, begets a particular kind of terrifying alienation, for the simple reason that we forfeit our ability to love when we place commodities above our fellow men. And someone who cannot love is always alone.

These hostile forces have often compelled poetry to burrow deeper into itself; it has retreated into its shell of obscurity and isolation. In such precarious times, writing poetry is always a defiant gesture that poets make against power and money, insensitivity and terror. Poetry cannot help anyone to get on in life, or make a successful human being out of anyone. But poetry should move us; it should change us in such a manner that we remain no longer the same after we've read a meaningful poem. For all these reasons, a poet can never be a conformist. He may not be an anarchist, a nihilist, or an inquisitor, but by the token of his verse, he is a natural dissident.

Czeslaw Milosz questions the efficacy of poetry in his 'Dedication': 'What is poetry which does not save/Nations or people?/A connivance with official lies/A song of drunkards whose throats will be cut in a moment.' But he will also not espouse his native language or champion his people's cause unquestioningly. As he says in 'My Faithful Mother Tongue':

Now, I confess my doubt.
There are moments when it seems to me I have squandered my life.
For you are a tongue of the debased,
Of the unreasonable, hating themselves
Even more than they hate other nations,
A tongue of informers,

A tongue of the confused,
Ill with their own innocence.

Poetry is always an act of subversion. And paradoxically, the poet is perhaps the most ironic realist. No more for him the security of an ivory tower or the temptations of Utopia. In 'Who Is a Poet', the Polish writer and poet Tadeusz Różewicz offers with certitude an ambivalent definition:

> a poet is one who writes verses
> and one who does not write verses
>
> a poet is one who throws off fetters
> and one who puts fetters on himself
>
> a poet is one who believes
> and one who cannot bring himself to believe
>
> a poet is one who has told lies
> and one who has been told lies
>
> one who has been inclined to fall
> and one who raises himself
>
> a poet is one who tries to leave
> and one who cannot leave

Each word must be fashioned from a private hurt, and writing poetry is like trying to keep a deadline with death. 'Perhaps I am always dying/Yet I listen willingly to the words of life/that I have never understood' wrote Quasimodo. That is why I've always felt that poetry should not merely amuse us or make us think: it should comfort us, and it must heal the heart of man.

—Robin S. Ngangom

WORDS AND THE SILENCE

(1988)

Homeland I Left

Homeland I left on an adolescent's sultry day,
why do you keep your distance?

I cannot recall your night's intimate tongues
or blend living voices with names.
The child's aroma of your dewy earth eludes me,
and native women are unwilling
to sleep in my dream's bed.
Cousin Joy died young. Friend Tomba
still in prison. Do you remember
mother-naked we muddied
our lukewarm river which gave us sores in return?
Or how we staged our truant plays,
in a bushy haven on our hillock, smoking
bidis, playing dirty innocent games?

And how much we loved the garish festivals
or catching fish from stagnant pools.
You would fight on your sharp machete streets,
but we were young, and curious of women.
We also flew glass-teethed kites, planted exotic flowers,
and hatched chickens with delinquent bodies,
hunted small game in rice fields, and
galloped through every lane of Imphal on bicycles,
making passes at almost every girl.

I hear a wicked war is now waged on our soil, and
bloody bodies dragged unceremoniously
though our rice fields, that they have dropped
the word 'shame' from everyday parlance, and
the newly-rich are ruling our homes.

I hear that freedom comes there only
when escorted by armed men.

To a Valley Known as Imphal

Red flaking bricks and mortar of palaces, buried rivers
and humiliated freedom fighters from the Great War
bring to mind

a king who tried to evade an ominous prophecy
only to be bitten by a snake-god
and two lovers
hailing from different faiths
embracing each other across the banks
of a cleaving river
in a small land-locked valley.

My departed grandmother
told stories of
bomb-hollowed walls and Japanese soldiers
who vanished in the jungle with someone's rice-pot
and Negroes from the Allied Forces
who tried to molest an aunt.

Whatever happened to all the mislaid years
no one cares.

When the bombs rained
my people ran in all directions
hugging mountain slopes, trampling rice-fields.
Many perished in bewilderment

but the war was not ours and
our race did not perish.
We have become civilized
in lieu of a barbaric past.
One cockcrow we found
ourselves belonging to
a country freed at midnight.

From the Land of the Seven Huts

Although we put down trees all season
in our highlands, branches held out as our guileless hands,
the rainsong like our troubled dreams
drumming up pride now on roofs, yet muffled by shame
and retreating into our solitary slopes, will linger
until late fall, hence our fates are forever
swathed in sheets of winter rain.

We of the hills who have so little
will we be patient with the voices of our women?
With the munificence of our trees, with our widowed fields
and hounded animals?

What is this wound we lanced ourselves and
drew blood where no blood was?
Who brought this unrest of dialects,
a foreign ensemble of music and dances amongst us
who once honoured the same forest-gods and
poured mutual libations of rice-wine?

Our roosters have no sense of dawn and, startled, crow
even as we sleep, deceived by moonlit nights,
while on our mornings the beasts they harnessed
in the plains mockingly roar at our divided huts.

Will we still sit back in smoke-laden longhouses,
sling the mechanical birds and
not be ashamed of our tribal desires?
And as a man takes birth, will we not
always lend him a clan name which
he will honour and die with?

Let our travel-fatigued eyes
drink once more from our succulent springs.

Khamba of Moirang

It was Khuman Khamba of Moirang
who told Thoibi that he is only one woman's
in all of the land, and
when she asked of this enviable one,
Thoibi the dewdrop poised on a lotus bud,
Thoibi of the plantain-limbs,
Khamba pointed one steady finger
to her own face of many moons
mirrored in the placid eyes of Loktak lake.
And the doe-eyed Thoibi could only utter,
'Oh, it is she then.'
Khamba the orphan, the tall long-haired silent one,
Khamba of the bamboo-groves,
who yearned for nothing but only
the princess he loved.

And because leaves do not rustle
without a wind, as fiery embers
cannot be kept covered by a cloth,
their love reached every lip of Moirang.
until Chingkhu Naha Tellheiba, Thoibi's father,
Chingkhuba the crown prince, furious and
vain as a raging storm, decreed
Khamba's painful and loveless death.

A Poem for Mother

(after Salvatore Quasimodo)

Palem Apokpi, mother who gave birth to me,
to be a man how I hated leaving home
ten years ago. Now these hills
have grown on me.
But I'm still your painfully shy son
with a ravenous appetite,
the boy who lost many teeth
emptying your larder. And
I am also your dreamy-eyed lad
who gave you difficult times
during his schooldays, romancing
with every girl he met, even
when he still wore half-pants.

You told your children that
money and time do not grow on trees.
But how does one ever learn to use them?
It isn't that I've forgotten
what you've come to mean to me
although I abandoned so much, and left
so little of myself at home
to remember me by.

I know how you work your fingers to the bone
as all mothers do, for unmarried sons,
ageing husband and liberated daughters-in-law.
Worried about us, for a long time
your lips couldn't flower into a smile,
lines have furrowed your face and
the signs of snow are on your hair.

Today, as on every day, you must have risen
with temple bells before cockcrow, swept
the floors and after the sacred bath,
cooked for the remainder of us. I can see you
returning every dusk from the bazaar,

your head laden with baskets.

Must you end toiling forever?
I'm sorry Palem.
I've inherited nothing
of your gentle ways or culinary skills.
Forgive me, for all your dreams
of happiness during your remnant days,
I only turned out to be a small man
with small dreams.

Ode to Hynniew Trep

Solitary light
on far eastern hills,
soft rivulet,
evening bells,
wistful widow,
forgotten rambling rose
poised
for the renegade.
The wind plays
on your *duitara*.

Faraway green and
brown rolling rug,
heart-woven gentle woollens
of rain and fog,
but fickle drencher,
lover's sky,
raindrop
slivering in the eye.

Hills with spires of churches,
hills with rice-terraces for siblings,
hills with laden steps
where tribes of earth mate.

Woman with pine hair,
girl with orchid breasts,
woman with mouth of plum,
girl with feet
of shining stone.
Slim hip of hill resorts
with misty loin-cloth,
cool descending
stream of trees
to rainforests
darker than night.

Shimmering cascade,
nude twilight
reposing on eyes,
living root bridge
of arterial rivers.
Crucible of hearts.
Deep-burning
ancient rice-wine.

Weekend

The man returns home drunk, late Saturday night
ascends the steps, floorboards creaking.
He bangs at the door, shouting at the woman.
Bleary-eyed, the woman opens the door.
Once inside, the man picks up an argument with the woman.
He says the woman doesn't love him.
He says she treats him badly and on purpose.
The woman replies without stop.
The man starts berating, then manhandling the woman,
rather gently, not violently,
as if he's dusting a costly vase,
afraid to break her.
The woman bawls in the inert, humid night.
The children start crying loudly too.
'Our mummy's dead, she's done for!'
The man can hold himself no longer.
His face goes all green.
He vomits noisily all over the place.
He starts whimpering too.
Suddenly, the man rushes out in the muggy night.
The woman rushes after him.
From somewhere on the calm road she drags him back.
The woman cleans up.
After a while, all is silence.
The man is heard snoring later.
Another Saturday drops from the calendar.

In the morning, the man teases the woman in bed.
The woman, not angrily, but rather pleasantly, says:
'Please stop, not in front of the children.'
They share a smoke. After a while the woman gets up.
She goes to the kitchen and sings
A popular film song. But she has forgotten the lyrics.
So she makes up her own meaningless lines.
She starts cooking with the children.
The man belches loudly after lunch.
In the afternoon, the man goes out,
the woman with him, their arms coupled.
They are dressed in their Sunday best.
The children are left playing in the yard.
They want candies on a Sunday.

This weekend is spent.

Hynniew Trep

When some sojourner who stayed takes away
the memory of a tremor and where the tar ends
poverty starts walking unclothed from the dirt road,
spilling as aged rice-wine until it finds sanctuary
in the cascades and unfastened raven hair of your women.

Denuded, sweet-smelling hills, it is here
among your boulders and pines that thatched huts
will lie with stone mansions, and the material hand
poised on the trigger is forever betrothed
to the artisan and peasant who have little.

Each trembling heart here harbours a caged passion
that threatens to wreck its keeper.
I felt them stop beating at times to germinate again
from the sour ashes of last night's drink, and
lovers reconcile with an affirmation of infants.

Seven Huts of my solitude, my first love,
your rain, your wind, searched my face for signs
of guilt when I first disembarked, a fugitive
fleeing from bonds of blood and ambition.
You who harboured me like a shame, and
demanded my consistency.
I saw the years clutched within
your arms of dwindling pines,
pleading with your errant people to return.

This is how the essence of dreams
latch on to the city's will-o-the-wisp.
But I've remained and watched your hours
drip in rain and glimmer in the distance.
The lips of your women are dark red
as your wine of cherries, even as they heap
a deep thirst on my lips.

To Poetry

It was for the gift of words
that I went in search of you,
pure, anonymous woman,
with hope you'll show the way
to a famished mendicant and
another drifting soul farer,
in fear none can fill the emptiness
that threatens to collapse
into a black solitude.

I inverted each fallen leaf hoping
to find you tangled in dark river-beds, or
a city's impenetrable rooms,
flowering on autumn boughs
away from an apostate's hands, or
caught in a hunter's web, and
wanting to free you so that you would
aim like an arrow towards my withering heart.

I have walked stubble fields
of elevated earth, hoping to waylay you
with nude worship once you return,
homeward bound with mateless wings, and
pitcher around your waist, flowering
among yellow mustard with fleeting promises
in your eyes, of bright river clay, faceted lips,
when sunlight is flung across the shores
of a languid river.

Again and again I heard your name
in the muezzin beckoning the faithful
tremble in the early fog
lying about a lonely city, your faraway voice
dissolving as bells from rustic temples.

I who grew restless dallying with lukewarm waters,
weary of repetitive winds, I who unearthed
the meaning of woman to man,
know you wait there shimmering
at the edge of all my circling dreams.

Evening

Hazy evenings float in the hills,
copper-coloured leaves
falling on earth's perimeters
from a day's stunted tree.

Such evenings and years returning
with a fury to engrave the mind's almanac
inked in the limpid eyes of reproach.

How long shall we burden our homes,
we who can no longer remember
what it means to be loveless?

Young woman often met,
with long questioning eyelashes.
Of what might have been
we shall never speak.
I cannot ask what you will avail
by opening my night
with glistening breasts and
emptying joy.

Out here, on fringes of wishes,
stars burn on the sky's
revolving forehead.

The Quest as Beginning

And what will we find
before the passing of our race,
we who search endlessly, upturning bones,
mixing ashes and not letting the dead sleep?
We seek answers alone, look for signs and curatives,
in our small sky-weary valley, barricaded by mountain ranges,
guarded by mountain-men, but do not reach the sea
which will reduce us to silence, or scale snow-capped peaks
to help us meditate.

Let us only speak of what reached our ears.
In Kangleipak, once beneath a time,
the royal beast of Kangla bit his tail, and
the land lay snug within his coils, and
there was no dearth of earthly things.
Fish teemed in waters and in fields
ears of rice danced to the season's drums.
From the minstrel's song at the dead of night
we heard winter yarns of warrior-kings
who reassured the land and children of no fear,
of men with untiring sword-arms.
We were sung of extraterrestrial maidens
who descended on earth and vanished;
Ingellei and Kombirei, elusive wild flowers,
who fell before their lovers could wear them,
telling that in banishing love
we only banish ourselves.

We heard whatever is not lost.
We speak of our blood's memory.

Let us also speak of what we found.
In the place of gold-dust we found
golden ears of rice under the dying year's copper haze,
swaying to the valley's wind-plucked music,
beacons of wildfires we saw on dry autumn nights,
mountains signalling the fate of trees and grass.
Instead of pages of heroic feats or undying love,
we read parchments written in blood, our history
indelibly stained with illicit love, with betrayal;
we found our alphabet buried with shrunken heads
of enemies and ghosts who died long ago,
laughing at the attempts at civilization.
Just beyond the ramparts of the cultured city
we found only the crumbling flesh of corruption,
not dances, music, or poetry
but generations of groaning slaves.

And we saw the faded words inscribed on its walls:
'There is antidote for snakebite,
There is no antidote for the bite of man.'
From us who failed and cannot die
we pass on to you who continue the journey
only our relentless dreams.

The Dead Shall Mourn the Living

See the shadow-lips behind lace curtains
watched from the street; the impenetrable windows
and the sorrowing virgins silhouetted
by mute lamps; see the hurried clocks
between adulterous lovers and
the sheepish debris on walls.

How many times have we seen
fire wilting in crystal brown eyes and
a slow cataract of hate forming?

Look, childhood has died for that urchin.
He now lights his *bidi* in the dark noon and
bears a filial cross on his hunched back.

The end touches us momentarily.
Its voices, its skeletal fingers,
its bone-chilling hoarfrost blanketing
yesterday's hill.
Life filters through our bodies,
its gauze wings eluding our enclosing fingers.
It is no precious stone
we can hold and admire in the sun.

See that tramp from my native land.
He has survived with only the wet streets
beneath his shoes-bereft feet.
He has no pillow to lay his head,
no fire to cook or warm himself and
he just beds down among obsolete machines.

The dead shall mourn the living.
Never knowing who is better-off.
Mutually shaking their heads
in shadow-pity.

TIME'S CROSSROADS

(1994)

Fog

May ends in regret.
To see houses, the town, headstones
wear the grey wrap of the fog, and
hearts, less than two now,
leaving the restless street
to walk iridescent lanes, taking time
in the desired drizzle in your face.

More than even love itself,
the thought of loving is better.
Memories can be picked, and
in wind and rain
I cannot think of you as apart
from laughter and hearths.

To see only our ghostly selves embrace and
kiss from remembrance among pines, dark with rain,
drink warm wine in haunted restaurants and
melt in the fog to be born again.

To be mapless lovers from the past
and be ghosts with fingers of rain.

I At the End of Autumn Sitting Near the Window

It is the ninth moon and already
a shiver runs down the back of the hill.
In calm solitude I latch my door,
wondering if I'll ever see
plum blossoms again.

Blinking among pines the autumn stars.
Silk-spun moonlight and
silver stream breaking over stones.
Laden peasants from day's end
bringing winterwood to the *Syiem's* mansion.

How sad is the lot of my friend Manik,
spilling his heart
from the seven mouths of his flute,
even though he has dared to wear
the flower of the *Syiem.*

II Spring at Ri Bhoi

Winter withdraws quietly from the Ri Bhoi hill.
Like white wreaths to deck the late year's coffin,
peach blossoms fall in spring wind.

Swept clean by March wind the hills,
fog melting from the nestling hamlet and
green are the pines skirting it.
Laughing children on their way to meadows,
men and women with ploughs
before the industrious season.

Because life falls as petals and
death comes when least expected,
none remembers the passing of Manik Raitong
and how he planted his bamboo flute
for earth to play music in spring.

But cold cold is the *Syiem's* heart and
spring has not visited his garden.

These two poems use a popular Khasi story of star-crossed lovers. U Manik Raitong (the Wretched), an orphaned youth, had an illicit affair with the king's (Syiem's) wife. When the affair came to light, the king's council decreed U Raitong's death. An accomplished musician, U Raitong planted his bamboo flute in the earth before his immolation. It is believed that the bamboo flute took root.

Lessons

After things I have learnt,
solitary puzzles I solved,
I stand in the shade
of reminiscent trees and think
about surrendering pretensions.

But disillusion bites the tongue, and
yesterdays uncovered their weathered faces,
of fleeting women and men
enacting desire
on the wet friezes
of rain-beaten memory.

It all began
with the sad sonatas
conducted by earth and sea, and
nights fell in monotony
with an illusion of evenings,
bringing unease and copious tears,
moistening lips and throats
with origin-less fears of betrayal
and pointless embraces.

There were strangers here, and
ego sitting heavy on their heads,
who skulked away
after sowing their rash seeds.
There was love locked out,
shouldered from the hearth and
left to shiver outside.
There were straitlaced lies and
gullible bodies crumpling,
a trifling with dreams, and old men
rudely reminded of humiliating youth.
There were fatherless girls
whose fiancés were stolen
by their own mothers, and
much talk of buying and selling.
There were drunken words
scribbled on dirty floors,
about love when mouths met and
treachery when lips were left alone,
with an unending talk of intangibles.
There were boys trying to be men, and
men who were enchanted into dogs.
There were old friends who merely nodded
from chauffeured cars, and gossip
on streets, doled out as truth.

There was hard maidenhood
preserved with escorted kisses, and
easy girls trying to borrow virginity
for a solitary night.
There were happy widows hiding
tears in heart-shaped urns, and
rich women comforted
for the most impertinent pain.
There were variations of the same day,
the same rain and laboured winters.

For all this
I'm redefining the night,
after losing things I loved most.
I'm recalling fevers and contortions
without the least understanding.

Hill

Hill, the ancient ones speak of a time
when the gods, tired of heavens,
descended to earth, and with lustful fingers dipped in
primeval clay, moulded your torso and breasts.
They scooped the clouds and
poured them over diaphanous cliffs
to fashion your silver hair.

With subterranean instincts
you have seen habitations, and
generations of children come and go.

When you descend in green bends to the town
you bring garments of fog, mushroom hampers,
rare flowers and wild birds,
until the day I died and took birth
in your sanctified woods.

During the festive season when the cold
gathers holly leaves, and
lips of boys and girls meet in benison
I felt as lonely as you and heard your voices,
pipes and maidens and
foxes barking in the distance.

Hill, you have preserved from ruin
hearts like mine, becoming lost
with civilization's shoes, for clouds
come home as they find you.

From 'The Book of Grievances'

I

From here, day weeps in the failing light
and the evenings are misty-eyed.
The eaves drip pastoral dew.

Dark green are leaves of June,
hung on the clothesline of rain.
The hills remain impassive
with an old reputation of silence, and
none knows about our dreams
muffled now as if by blaring progress,
put to shame before ornate streets.

In the evenings proud hearts
that have learnt to die well
return in the bronze dusk.
But something has been buried,
something akin to hope, and dreams.

Our souls shall not speak.
Not an indignant word
shall escape our lips, and
if they cannot hear
the silent moan of our hearts
we will not implore pity.

Implacable death came upon us, and
the finest memories are of no worth;
proud ancestral names, faithful women
with raven hair, the heroic struggles
of our small lives.

What is our tradition and our history
but only death with a long memory?
For how long shall we make
Our forefathers walk as spirits?

Today, with grief sitting on our hearts
we will sing of clouds that did not come home,
we will sing the songs of those banished in mountains,
we will drink deep from bamboo mugs, and
wipe remembrance from our lips.

From a trajectory of dark deeds
our days fly toward destinations
in uncharted galaxies of time.

II

Broken skylines clutch the hills
bringing a momentary fear
of the earth-shaker
who turns violently in his sleep.
As we sauntered along overgrown trails
the hill's night sang to us,
but concealed its myths
of famine and pestilence.

A party of egrets followed us
in the fog one January morning.
When we stole into the fog's body
we again entered our history,
leaving all milestones behind.
In these native villages, beneath the bamboo
and watching hills, seated on mats of clouds
we could see the glint of paddy-fields
gripped by rain and mist.
Once we sprinkled mutual libations
to create these jade and emerald fields.

My love, something I cannot name
seems to be ashamed of our dances.
Even as we hide our roots like gnarled limbs,
we begin to disown what we cherish:
fidelity, openness, daring. We must learn
quickly, before the devious ones mutilate
our names carved on monoliths.
Time ran out in Oinam, in Ukhrul,
when they who gave us a republic,
brought *reconcentrados* from the Americas,
watched impassively the smoking fields,
prodded with clubs the bruised vagina,
the shocked testis. We became
impotent in the face of mortification.

Today, we will bury tradition's foetus.
We will not weave unparalleled history
where there was no homespun yarn. We
the worthy henchmen of tyranny
will embrace the villain's principles.
We will desert honour and a vain hope
for peace will burn our hills.

When we scream and our throats rasp
we will spit wanton civilization in the eye.
As east meets west in the hills' crack
blind venous roots grope under earth.
We turn our own perpetrator,
victim of our own dark deeds.

It is all very fine
long-sacrificing brother of the night,
your state-of-the-art rifle commands awe.
When you procure your ignominious arsenal
can you smother the sibilant whispers
in the valley and the hills, can you
answer the cries of children and widows?

You singed the flower of youth
with the pious lamp in your veins.
But our homes have been herded away
for our fields to lie fallow, and
our young and old spread maimed hands
for the intractable belly, the naked skin.

Imphal

I

Nothing has changed in this backdrop.
Boys with earrings
enter hairdressing saloons and
set their hair with dirty combs;
the maimed women with meager leaves
in the bazaars imploring pity,
the men lording over them;
and the girls everywhere,
spying from balconies,
on display with renovated faces
in streets, in colleges,
happy as beauty queens and then
the boys again, proud to drive their fathers' cars.
But outdoing them all
the drug-fiends,
with bodies alive and
eyes dead.

This is the ancestral ground
of the Meiteis.
A lottery of souls
is held here every day.
Sons, daughters,
with strength of elephants,
your homeland is on fire.

II

I find winter each year
when I return like a dead ritual
to this gnarled land.
Here, I am both native and illegal migrant.
The minister is my shepherd,
I shall not want.
Yeah, though I walk
in the valley
in the shadow of Aids,
I will fear no man.

III

There is something sadly inevitable
about this land, something inescapable,
like a beast which stalks its own death,
like an ominous prophecy
of men clad in red going to war,
like an arrow when released
seeks the man who strung the bow.

Today, when everything seems to be
pointing again to prospect and fortune,
when no longer the minion of Empire
the fantasies of capital have come true,
when our arts strut in the streets,
when the entire nation recognizes us,
when our poetry is filled with paeans
of pluck and progress,

when our culture is put up for display,
something sinister sours
our fondest dreams.

IV

Land of my childhood
I can no more pretend to love,
where I heard the bicycles
leaving in the morning and
a kitchen warm with smells.
I can be found hidden in a corner,
the soft boy with a fondness for epics
as some rowdy friends
plan the conquest
of a neighbouring territory;
one galloped a stolen horse
through a crowded bazaar
cutting the throng to pieces and
walked on to become
the marksman
of a subversive outfit.

I should have been there
to keep track of hidden paths
that lead to the jungle,
the mazes that weave the heroic lore.
I should have monitored
the boys shot down and
counted the soldiers
they ambushed.

I should have been there
in a deserted hamlet in Ukhrul
when every able-bodied male
fled to the nearest jungle and
only naked children
were left playing
with stolid old women.

Myanmar's Story

That country where I return in memory to dim travels
of a child, where serpentine roads
of a long war send me to its twilight borders,
to its fair women with raven hair and sandalwood breasts,
its poor rice-fields and hills rain-bound, and
monasteries old in wisdom,
that journey was made some time ago
as only wishfulness would allow.

Once, a poet-explorer from equatorial distances
with unknown blood singing in his heart, walked
its streets, marvelled at its strange gods,
loved anxiously and discovered loneliness.
But these are darker days, my love,
when freedom has become a rare metal
that must be mined from cruel intelligences.
There is nothing more bitter than hearts of men
without a country, more terrible than the exile
of young men and women who only want
to make their people see with words not guns,
pleading with indifferent countries, protesting
with colours and alphabets
against a 'senseless crushing of flowers'.

I'm telling the story of Myanmar and its brave daughters
deserted by the big brothers of the West, and
democracy weeping in its tropical forests,
I speak of incessant tears hidden in the folds
of intoxicating freedom. Listen, love,
to Burma's story, once the East's pearl, now
the bauble of democracy, the elusive
white man's cross that natives carry, causing
its physicians, students and priests to mourn
their native land's fate, to sing fugitive songs
around the world, hoping only songs will preserve
fragile sanity in a mad country where bandits
come riding in tanks to greet its citizens, generals
enslaved by their own horrors, purging their terrors
by uprooting fields and gardens, exterminating
before things could grow into nightmares.

My love, in my dream where they tear a green
heart from the hill's ribs in steamy jungles
for the idle whites swooping on Rangoon, who
will take away jade souvenirs to remind themselves
of a subject race, I carried you across slopes
of my war-torn mind, leaving furrows of lead and
put flaming orchids in your bridal hair.
In my dream each drop of blood sprouts
a humming voice the bandits throttled.
But the running blood grows in clamour,
answering unerringly to new voices.

Guidebook

(after Derek A. Walcott)

In winter huts huddle
in the cold of feudal terrain
and the man of the hills
still sits, toils, and dreams
in the incomprehension of festering progress
of ugly concrete and feverish towns
of these Northeastern colonies.
Tear up your passports
when you arrive here.

Natives as grasping as the nationals
of independent India,
girls to be had by the conquistador salesman,
we are a Babel of colourful tribes
selling indigenous culture
in these worlds you would discover
in Encyclopedia Britannica
and brochures for tourists.
But when the burrower
from the tough plains
thinks of our gullible hills,
he should remember
that we who seem uncouth
will also bite the hand which feeds.

Goan Sketch

(for Leo Cordeiro)

In Panjim
the festive lights of the Carnival
across the river, ferried us to a dream
which entered our eyes, like jewels
studding the navel of the dancing night sky.

As the ferry churns the dark waters
music greeted us in the balmy air.
What do the songs tell?
Of gentle fisherwomen on anxious sands
sea lapping their feet?
While almond eyes sweep the curved horizon
do they await a night's ecstasy?
The dances speak of emerald fields
and natives bent double
stooping to replace the earth's bounty.
And at Miramar's edge
Gasparides keeps vigil
for Paula's imminent return,
the lights in her eyes guiding his hurricane heart.

When red cotton flowers and magnolia
arouse the wanton winds of Bardez
church bells toll for prodigal sons
to return to the fold. As bazaars
laden with exotic merchandise
spill once more
at riverside and seashore.

We toast cups
of mysterious dark-bodied wine
to the land and the sea.

Amid palm fronds
the sea will be kissed by stars tonight.
And we've come from faraway hills
to carry the sounds of the sea with us.

I Walk the Khasi Winter Sunlight

(*after Dennis Brutus*)

I walk the Khasi winter sunlight
and see something akin to hope
turning the cherry trees
with an old grief returning.

When violent blood sleeps under winter earth
unrelenting youth retraces it steps
on winter's street with a lover's swagger
and I watch beauty from a careful distance
outlined on December's warm meadows
their laughter woven in the wind.
I hear again the merry guitar
and church bells ringing for the erring sons
and see the custodians of justice
inside their polished gods,
on their composed visages an unreal light.

And I think of the hills' imprisoned evenings,
and the boys far from home squatting in their cells,
in their breasts hope fading
and grim embers burning their eyes,
their days an empty platter
their nights a dark shroud.
And I think of their captors
feeding the meals of hatred,
and their mothers awaiting their return
their faces veiling the mottled colour of fear,
and only lugubrious drums beating in my heart.

THE DESIRE OF ROOTS

(2006)

Primary Schools

I remember only the detritus of schools
which taught fear,
where nuns alone seemed to believe
in the power of the written word and punishment.
There was a boy in the middle of it all
who once forged his father's signature
in order to dodge a maths test and
spent the whole day in a World War II cemetery
sleeping between roses and epitaphs.
The intimidation of books from Glasgow
made him steal small notes and coins from his father
which admitted him to a mystic circle
of titbits, cannabis, and adult tales
far away from pink rooms and uniform handwriting
or 'eena meena maina mo' by rote
after clambering walls of desolate afternoons
to the freedom of cork trees and frogs and egrets,
a stinking marshy world of catapults and running noses
which grappled with black polished shoes and
moral science, to return home on overcast dusks
brewing storm-aroused nights, only to be
exiled on a reed mat with a hurricane lamp and
slate, chalk, and as the years grew up
inkwell and bamboo-pulp paper became
the keepsakes of his childhood.
There were mosquito storms and
cool dirt floors polished with cow dung and clay,
lizard myrtles and moss trained on walls

which reminded elders of neglect
near a big water tank left behind by British soldiers
where vipers came to drink, and
gaudy walls of curvaceous goddesses.

I can see the naive boy
who couldn't read the dirty word
spelt on the ground by his older friends
in the calligraphy of randy boyhood,
and, later, obsessed with that moist idea
explored his girl cousins fervently.

There were long delightful, convalescent afternoons
of illustrated classics without
the stress of the school bus when he heard
only the sleepy clang of hammers
in the nearby smithy, when day burnt slowly
like calories even when he was sleeping,
without the solemnity of anyone's life
coming to an end.

Poetry

What they don't need is poetry,
these gnarled men and wrinkled women
who work the slopes,
swaying in the rain like knotted,
weather-beaten pines, breathing
mountain air, these weavers and herdsmen.

What matters if I can't explain to them
the nuance of an ode or a ghazal,
the iron and flint of an Akhmatova
or a Guillén, how do I impress upon them
their miserable plight
when all they want to do
is smoke and chatter away time?

When he hears poetry
the peasant will lean on his hoe
in exasperation while his fields lie fallow,
the hunter will return empty-handed with
a sad poem, and if the goatherd listens
to poetry's demented cadences
his goats will not give milk.

Let me explain.

Like the great poets
pardoned by time
I wanted to gather words
from arrows nocked in a turquoise sky.
I wanted to catch words in my embroidered bag,
rainy words spattered, thrown about
by the March wind, I wanted to collect
pebbly words from riverbeds, smooth,
geometrical consonants of primary colours.
I wanted to unearth roots and herbs
and compound a word-salve, I wanted
to forge words on an anvil.
I've always wanted to be a wordsmith.

The sweeper wakes up the morning without irony.
I want him to burn my anxieties and not
sweep them under the mat as I used to.
I want the carpenter
to fashion me a word-chair
to sit me down and calm me,
I want him to nail me down a poem.
The carpenter has learnt his trade and cannot
waste hours chiselling and planing couplets.
I wanted the mason to lay
the cornerstones of living for me.
The mason awaits cargoes of sand and bricks
on the shores of afternoon and doesn't need
silken rhetoric or spiced adjectives.

All I wanted was to sing
with the mystical sparrows,
but only a murder of crows
nest in my throat at dawn.
I wanted to harvest words
which grow on their own, words
which die without tawdry funerals;
of creepers and vines, stars and stone,
wisdom and folly, flowers and moss.

To a Woman from Southeastern Hills

Woman with the soft voice
whispering wind in the trees
I know why you run away from me,
fading from leaf to hill,
pursued by my tarnished name.
I who was born at an unearthly hour,
a sibling of light and darkness,
a freak among practical men,
a composer of bitter verse.
But you only tossed your riverine hair and
earth moves again on its wistful axis,
while a river flows hushed in an underground heart.

You, woman, from Southeastern hills,
cloud-covered mystery, gliding on rain,
deep drink of rice wine with eyes closed,
child of the dancing bamboo, unction
of ginger on the wagging tongue.
Your voice is soft because mountain streams
taught your heart.

Tonight, a full moon steals above northern pines,
and boys from your native land sit on terraces
with their dolorous guitars, singing of loves
lost in the ravines of the heart.
I am that plaintive cry you did not wish to hear,
the love song you've exiled.
Even now my dreams sprout wings

among our impassive people, circling
in the storm with sad pride and faraway months,
ready to die and be trampled in mud.
In you, woman, from southeastern hills
all our memories gather into trembling hopes,
taking us back to a time before they gave us
religion to divide us, before the politician-priests
who sacrificed for their own redemption,
mouthing the name of god among benighted heathens.

Time before science, civilized laws and rock music,
time in the memory of gods.
Before coat and before nylon, bare-bosomed time,
time of the *puan** and story-telling cloak,
the running motif caught by fabric,
eloquent bead encircling your slender neck.
You, woman, on your father's terrace, a loom
hugging your hips, singing with the dancing
shuttle in your hand, you offered me tobacco.
In afternoons you return with water humming
in the bamboo and asked if I were thirsty.
That was the time of the weretiger, before
temples and churches, time of the freethinking
dormitory, when boys trained in the school of
the warrior, time of the daring headhunter,
when legends could not wait to be born, and
places were named. And time before this
English tongue we speak now.

Forgetfulness of being afflicts us.
Let us refuse these names, woman,
our names we proudly put down on pages,
these names that come between our lips
cold as parchment. They can never learn
our songs, or feel the drumbeats of our hearts.
How would they harness the rivers
in our blood, rushing without boundaries,
or tame our precipices and sullen fields?

Will you, woman, devastate these dreams
as men ravage the hills, leaving only
scars and litter behind, after all hopes
have been mined? Woman, from the land
of Chhura,** our roots suck from the
same liquid tongue. Because of these
shared dreams and waters, none knows you
like I do. I who can nurture the twin syllables
of your name. Speak again, woman,
with your dulcet tongue, for this is the desire
of these hills and yearning stones.

*Puan: a traditional sarong-style dress worn by Mizo women.
**Chhura: the name of a popular Mizo folk-hero.

Age and Memory

You can be no more,
it would seem,
than memory taken to bed,
closing eyelids merely
till the glint of dawn,
after watching stars that fall
from space at midnight.

I ambushed you today.
You rose like a woman
from the waves,
rubbing dark sleep
to illuminate
the brown light of your eyes.
Your bare feet on wood
and your breath
stirring the afternoon
like the rains of June.

Your heart and mouth and eyes
say you are a woman.
You had not a word
of yourself, secreted
your wanton desires.
You only taught joyless lessons
of hardened fidelity,
retreating into the earth
you feel secure in.

Maternal earth,
generous and callous.
You untouchable then,
and invulnerable now;
all your instincts
rearranged with
your scattered hair.

Were I to trace
my name on your frosted mirror
you would quickly efface it with your breath.

Street Life

I've had decadence forced on me.
I let the rain waste my day, and arriving
at streets that do not even know my name
I take off just like that, waving to silhouettes,
buying drinks for anyone, even primates
for whom I have no great regard, hating the houses
which warn of dogs instead of welcoming me.

I allow the rain to flay desire's skin
after falling in lust with an assortment of women,
pursued by an obstinate heat, and
an old nose for adultery.
I covet the well-groomed bodies of vehicles
which thread through the eyes of the street,
before darting in and out of shops interspersed like snares,
choosing clothes and shoes which the manly discarded, and
even perfumes to throw off my real self.
Reaching barber's hideouts
I spend hours there in a trade union
with men who deal in a hairy business,
watching fingers that pick noses and
teeth in disgusting turn.
I let them fondle my head for a long time.

Until I reached the blind alley of night, and
I slowly uncovered myself
observing shops murdered before they were born,
listening to the dead orchestra of the street.

The Ignominy of Geometry

The ignominy of geometry,
the inability to evade angles and parallels.
Living, we have to suffer that mortification
which robs the sacrifice of joy
of much of its sheen.

One minute of patronizing certainty and
the boring man is a 'square'
but when our understanding's poor
someone's off on a tangent, and
that dark excitement we all secretly envy
is an eternal triangle,
or, when two people cannot agree (naturally)
they are diametrically opposed,
bowing again to geometry,
a language of precision
to measure our imprecise lives.

We were given a white emptiness and
left to our devices.
Wanting more from life than mere life
we tried to fill that emptiness
with lush pigments, beauty, purpose,
a finishing touch of children.

We went looking for subjects in time and space
creating moments under cherry trees, lifting glasses to youth,
but merely fulfilled reprise's oracle and
we speak of a wheel coming full circle.
The ignominy of geometry,
the inability to see beyond centres and triangles.

Even my love was flesh and blood
because I had put my mouth on her lips.
Yet a wheel's fortune disdained us and
we became two tiny points of light
on that white emptiness,
drawing unhappy parallel lines.

Poem for Samir

From the dark sun in your face, and
your smile which comes from
the restorative twin leaves
handpicked by your rugged people, and
a house with its tense walls,
with rooms about to confide; from your life
mixed with verse and shadow and
humdrum existence, with children
in the courtyard and a gate opening
yet closing; from your sleep foundering
on the reefs of night, your head shaped
like an island drifting from the
continent of reason, a key missing
to your books of poetry and your
open heart like a door, I hide
the night's fuddled evidence
in the sultry city where happy
consignments fail to arrive.
I could no longer wait for the end
where men from confused directions
meet for a while to vanish forever.
I fade into that distance, harking back
to open fields of rice, away from your exhausted
cough of factories and engines, touching
braided roads to reach the hills.

One day we shall be together again
without names, with the simple things
of earth, with plantain leaves, in months
free of Mondays, and days without thoughts
of women, with earthen pots and bamboo spoons.
One day we shall walk that road where
carrion-hunters have not desecrated memory.

You could not exorcise the demons of the mind.
Yes, they exist. Listen, I've also come from a
country where pregnant women were pierced
by abortive lead, and children were sometimes burnt
as offerings to dark gods,
I come from a country where they took our past and
returned them as terrible dreams.

To Pacha

To your uneventful death, Pacha,
the stones hurled at your demented name, and
the doors closed on your life
it is fitting that none mourn
the face of your memory they slapped;
from booze artist Pacha to lunatic Pacha.

There are no more tears to shed
in this withered country where they
kill pregnant women and children; its
nipples have long gone dry, and leering
death walks your homeland. And why should
anyone weep for your lonely alcoholic end?
Young boys and soldiers are butchering each
other by the dozen, in the hills, the angry
streets, day after day, and too many heroes and
villains are not worth remembering at all.
Death is callous, Pacha, in the land of your
innocent birth.

Consummate madman, unknown comrade,
you were the best of them all;
whether you logged the meteorological conditions
of your stricken town, pen dipped
in your drunken blood, or portrayed
old men hard of hearing. Breaking heart
of roots, savage lover no woman would tame,
existential hero and fiercely proud pauper.

You laughed yourself insane in the teeth
of the gathering storm.

Hovel-dweller amidst concrete and iron,
anachronistic mendicant, and embracer of
manuscripts in pounding rain, angry star
which burned in our skies, what were
your dreams? Reveal them a little for me,
anonymous brother. Poetry in your
homeland must die a natural death
when one must 'sew up his lips and
clog his ears with mud,' and to be a
man, first of all, you must sell yourself
to the highest bidder.

Immaculate madling with resplendent dreams,
you refused to sell them in your land
where villains strut as the pure in streets.
You only said: 'One's homeland is dear. I
have not seen all of this land. I have not
been able to tread the grass that grows there.'
For a long time the tramps and lunatics
beckoned you, and only they shall
honour your name.

Pacha Meetei (1943-1990), one of the finest Manipuri writers, died at the
age of forty-six. Hounded as a drunkard and a madman during his final days,
he died in extreme poverty.

Goodbyes

Goodbye, time's assassin,
waited patiently for us in the cold,
for words to run out, for
the finished and voiceless submission.
We only mouthed the timeworn
'we should have never met,'
but didn't have the courage
to crumble a handful of earth
over our buried-alive beginning.

So we survived.
Apart from each other,
without meeting,
setting up the illusion everywhere,
inviting further pain,
while our buried beginning
lived with the turning days
as trees spurning leaves and
coming into leaf, as children
who have lost childhood, like heretics
condemned by the inquisition of living,
fading and quickening again; as despair,
as tawdry happiness, and
like fainting memory at last.
As it should be,
as it has always been.

Until one day
out of our cherished sorrows
a willow tree ascended and
fed its weeping
to a river.

So we survived.
Waiting for the
decisive blow of the axe.

Shadows

We are but shadows of the great spirits
who come from myth, and
are but shadows themselves.

Before these shadows arrived
everything was void with a blinding light.
The streets rang with a sharp emptiness and
the houses groaned under the weight of silence.
The shops merely looked at each other and
the rooms became solitary isles,
while the hour's inaudible tolling
disclosed the great silence of creation.

But slowly they fall into place,
these shadows immovable like foundations
filling the emptiness with indistinct
memories of birth, of the pure day
of holding hands, of the first fight
to earn boyhood, and clothes bought
on a feast day, the painful flight
of the maiden kiss still hovering
in the air, of uninvited loneliness and
the sincere joy of fornication,
of happy illnesses and feet that move
to sweeten the blood.

Before these shadows arrived
everything was innocent.
As we meet them under their long gaze,
we turn slowly into disembodied things
while they brood over these words, and
like sundials, lengthen over pages
in late afternoons.

During Easter

Winter languishes in the street
like an old man who refuses to stir
when constellations swing ingeniously and
cherries turn red like the luminous
lips of girls eager for kisses.

The streets are only half-emptied,
not everyone has gone to witness
the resurrection of the son of god.

On Maundy Thursday no one washes
the feet of the poor
as the son of man washes
the feet of his automobile.

But the miracle is here on earth,
as flesh and blood celebrate
the wonder of meaningless life
in the acridness of tear-filled rain
falling from already sleepy skies.
And yesterday's bitterness fades
the moment you forgive every bastard and
whore, and only thanksgiving follows
the shock of being alive.

On Easter Sunday, walk in the wind
that lingers in your hair, or
stand immobile like a grey carving
in the public square
after squandering your last rupee on a bottle, and
laugh at the son of man who anoints his car.

Under Easter stars
listen to the haunted organ
lifting a ghostly hymn, and pray
with a Paschal candle in your heart
for the sorrow of the woman
shut out from a church.

A Libran Horoscope

Somewhere among earthbound stars it slept
curled up in its parchment skin,
muttering the story of the fool
who will backtrack one day
to his unbelievable superstitions, and
having consulted the world
will return pursued by many fears.
My horoscope slumbered, thoughtless,
on my mother's heirlooms.
It dozed among heady flowers
quiet in the warm darkness.

Childhood took place
free from mannish fears
when I had only my mother's love
to protect me from knives,
from fire, and death by water.
I wore it like an amulet.
Childhood took place
among moonflowers and sunstone,
in nakedness with the wind as your wet nurse.
Childhood took place
among fairies and weretigers
when hills were yours to tumble down
before they sheltered soldiers and
dreaded chambers of torture.
Childhood took place
when boys built fugitive fires and

talked only of women
until your friend adored a gun
to become a widowmaker.
Childhood took place
before you ate from any tree and
before grapes were suspended over your head.
Childhood continued
until a boy's fluid dream became flesh
by the grace of a fallen woman.

My horoscope fell from innocence and
lost its sleep.
It came out from my mother's closet and
could not remember
the fragrance of roses.
It changed hands with money and
began suspecting many people.
It is in my safekeeping now.

Laitlum

I treasure you for the jealousy you've hatched,
the afterglow that deceived me in your noontide arms.
I want you with the pain of a green luminosity
or the warm shock of the myrrh of pines,
choking back ambuscade passion
I want to be converted amongst houses kneeling
in the thick of firs of former lives,
randomly built without electricity.

Misted wine of the ravine's murmuring epilogue,
pasturage swaying with your body's indelicacy.
Before a spellbound audience of rustic animals
we're travelling invisibly from age towards youth.

When you sealed your fate to mine
I discovered roads we had misplaced,
dark wet in the twilight's excited face,
wayside stalls opening iridescent eyes,
watery fields newly laid in olive longing and see
wisps of happiness wafting down the pines.

Revolutionaries

I

Before they used terror when things got a little out of hand and people betrayed reactionary behaviour, revolutionaries had asked poets in their lower ranks to compose patriotic songs for a country, which cannot be found on any map. They would coerce nocturnal drivers of interstate buses to play tapes of one-act plays, which are designed to make unsuspecting passengers weep with patriotic shame. I know this for real, I grew up with revolutionaries. They had even asked me to translate a press release over the phone.

Before he became the sharpshooter of a revolutionary band my childhood friend smelled of straw and cattle, and then one day, he bridled a horse and rode it hard through a busy marketplace scattering customers and traders alike like straw in a gale. I was told that he buried a pistol in my cousin's backyard just before he went underground. Only after he came overground with the venerable title 'teacher', because Chinese masters trained him, did I meet him on the street and he smelled of designer clothes. He now keeps himself occupied with work contracted out by the public works department and once asked me if I was married. He has two wives, one of them an actor.

Before the crackling fire of revolution, which warms the hearts of boys, we sat in a circle and talked endlessly about oppressors and life in the jungle. Friends brought stories of the ordained, who survived on roots and eggshells. We looked at Che's hammock with longing and even mixed his cocktail but had no idea of when to dig a tank pit. When little books with a star and red skins appeared, it was too late for me. I had fallen in love, and although it broke my heart, my father sent me to another land with gentle hills, so I could read other books which would make me stand on my bourgeois feet.

II

When they are not around they become the butt of fun. The roving story then was of a wastrel who went home after midnight because he had wasted all his time with his layabout friends around a fire one winter night. He had to cross a walled house guarded by fierce dogs to reach his home. When the owner of the house who was woken up by the dogs asked, 'Who goes there?' the wastrel found his wits and replied, 'In the service of the motherland' in a solemn voice as one would expect a revolutionary to reply.

When they became arbiters after someone's duck was stolen or two women were fighting over one man, I stopped being furious with them.

You should write when you can still laugh at yourself and the world, before you give yourself up to revolution's despair.

Gangtok, February 1998

(*for Guru T. Ladakhi*)

I

Call of faraway snow in the eye of a wish.
When we contemplate your emerald tongue
quivering on pale sand and rock
we grow more weary of striving cities
and desultory roads. But you will
teach us to name the forest and the mountain,
indignant one, who will not wait.
Teesta, tell me the meaning of your name.

Like secretive men impelled by a sinuous love
we follow your scent when the flame of the forest
borrows a monk's robes and something shimmers
beneath the veil of the Himalayan sky
until you lift us on your fraternal lap
of flowers and stone, Gangtok.

II

Who are the artisans of wood that left
no names on the palace gate of the Chogyal?
A misty forest looks up the face of a sheer drop
where the king's men punished hardened criminals
tied up in sacks, by pushing them off this cliff,
so the stories insinuate. The royalty since then
has paid its price to a nation which humbled them

through treachery, so history moralizes. And this
is where a landslide took many by surprise.
A lanky building just slipped off
and lay on its face like a drunk,
and only the prayer flags
stand here to appease the difficult gods.
I look where the mountains keep their enigmatic silence
and climb stairs which lead to the doors of the sky,
and rain entered the afternoon without invitation.

III

5 a.m. one whisky-coated morning
and Khangchendzonga appeared, bust translucent
like a forgotten model, her face quickly
obscured by a cirrus of snow,
provoked by a jealous sunstone
cast on her proud forehead.
In the aquamarine afternoon
Rumtek turns slow prayer wheels
which cut across the axis of earth
to generate compassion for a cold-blooded world.
The Karmapa who fled Tibet
reconstructed this arabesque seat of learning
from adoration and spotless memory.
We remove shoes and enter a hooded door
to find butter statues meditating
in all the shades of earth.
Thus, flesh will melt one day
to yield the running colours of earth.
An intonation of monks

and the deep drone of drums
heighten the mystery of reincarnation each moment.
But what does one seek from the illuminate
if the wayward mind must be conquered first?
A grimy gap-toothed Tibetan comes begging
while young acolytes scurry to fetch water,
as the world of appearance marked time.
Adornment, renunciation, ego, alms,
where is there a life without desire?

IV

5 p.m. when evenings crumble from Himalayan snow
Gangtok folds us in her breast.
We leave melancholy outside Zam-den,
where positive elements converge,
and song and dance and poetry
find a home.

When You Do Not Return

When you leave your native hills
winter is merely a reminder
of all past winters, of all
the loves we lost, and there's none
to care for the old and infirm. All
the hospices have closed their doors.

Leaves no longer respond
to the alchemy of seasons,
and the heart lies fallow
expecting winter rain. Earth
has closed again like a woman
when you do not return, and dreams
turn to rust, the flame and the dew
cannot create art. Only lust breaks
on the branches of night, and men
wear hideous masks, the fragrance
of the wild rose is lost, and only
the flowers of the market are on sale.

The poet loses his metaphors
when you do not return, and he
merely repeats himself in the
dreadful arithmetic of the day.
The world knew me as happy when
you gave me your healing hand
and now ignores my grief because

you left. The murmuring river
is hushed as it loses its course
in a sunless kingdom.

When you leave your native land
messianic young men betray principles,
and there's no fire in their eyes.
In the streets students shout themselves
hoarse for newly-arrived patriots. The
right and the left have become synonymous,
and citizens garland only the thieves.
The man of god merely chants the
sanctimonious burlesque of prayers,
while the poor remain cold and naked
the preacher is warm and fed. When
you do not return dead waters breed
reptiles in our minds, gunfire reverberates
in the hills, and bullets sprout from
windows instead of geraniums. When you
do not return after the bloodthirsty purges,
flies swarm around limp flags. The barbwire
of the day encloses us as we enter the era
of the assassin.

When you leave your native hills
I can only speak of lost times,
and of sorrow and blood. And I write
these letters of winter, asking you
to return again to the hills, on
grey pages I send you happiness
because it has left my home.

Bad Places

Sometimes, through no fault of its own, a neighbourhood picks up a bad reputation. If you happen to visit it on a singularly uneventful day, you will find it roofed with a blue sky, and dark-green pines and bamboo stooping to kiss its dusty road. And although it is true that love was made in all its wintry houses and its dead have been buried in its unruffled graveyard, you would never guess how it earned such a vague hatred from outsiders. Perhaps one night, acting on a tip-off, a party of nervous paramilitary men shot a couple of teenage militants to rags at the gate of one of its unfortunate houses. What is truly ironic is the fact that the revolutionaries do not hail from this neighbourhood, they merely happened to be there during an ill-timed party. It is also entirely possible that a few men and women desperate to find witches and warlocks in an increasingly faithless age, forged themselves into medieval instruments and burnt down a house, which looked a little eerie in the moonlight, and killed a strange old man and his wife.

It has been called names—a hideout, for instance. They say the scars on its walls are bullet marks really. You would be advised not to court its women because the area grows dangerous after sunset. But such neighbourhoods continue to grow as if nurtured by misgiving.

Laitumkhrah

No one looks at dark memorials
standing through lonely rain, their heads
trusting the sky's emaciated shoulders,
no one will stop to look at the dead.

The greeting sparrows were snubbed in the morning,
and no one bothers about fresh loaves
walking about in dirty foam, or remembers
the madman who used to send messages to the sky
from the local post office.

This is the strange town
which has come up in the world, with its
shabby Saturdays and vulgar make-up, congested
with lips reeking of politics, its yellowing oranges
and shops opening their slow provocative eyes,
its streets with their cheap perfumery
perversely detaining suburbanite followers.

I want to go back to its winter, its monotonous
rain brushing the window pane, just because
it made much of a foolish boy who loved
to throw away its hours and knew its quiet cottages.
I want to walk its midnight to waiting straw beds,
through its gates opened by rain, and outrage
its sullen homes with an illicit love.

I want to return to its buried drinking nests
smelling of smoke and pathetic camaraderie,
anticipating their thrilling pastimes
arranged by the local police.

I want to dispute this town's memory,
and make it look for me in vain.

The Strange Affair of Robin S. Ngangom

I

I remember misplacing
a bronze bell
somewhere, sometime.
I left behind many untended hearths.
Rushing back, I discovered
something had changed me.

I can say
I am this or that,
that I envied the character
of water and stone.
As a boy I was made a sheep,
now I am enchanted into a goat
that the townspeople
enjoy driving to the square
with a marigold garland
between my horns.

At twenty-four
I invited myself to Bohemia.
The kingdom of Art,
where people never grow old,
was my affable neighbour.

Moved by curiosity,
I found myself lingering
backstage, where painted girls
and poor blind boys
came to do their parts.
In the evenings now,
I often mix my drink with despair.
Love, of course, made me entirely useless.
This is the story of my people.
We sowed suspicion in the fields.
Hatred sprang and razed the crops.
Now they go to gloating neighbours,
begging bowls in hand,
fingers pointed at each other.
Their incessant bickering
muffles all pity.

Our intentions are clear.
Slash and burn,
let fire erase all traces,
so that distrust cannot write
our murderous history.
Somewhere inside the labyrinth
we met, locked horns, and
went our feuding ways.
Our past, we make believe, is pristine
even as we reaped heads and took slaves.
When we write make-believe history
with malicious intent,
memory burns on a short fuse.

As boys return to Christmas,
escorted by hate and fear,
they take a circuitous route
to outwit an enemy
who will revel too much in the birth
of a merciful son. When these boys
reach home, their dreams will come
dressed in red.

II

Hands filled with love,
I touched your healing breasts.
Like the beaten-up past
scars appeared on your body.
I ask, who branded the moon's skin of my love?
Who used you like a toy doll?
Only my hands disappear and return to me
mutilated with guilt.

When I turn with a heavy heart
towards my burning land,
the hills, woman, scream your name.
Soldiers with black scarves
like mime artists
turn them in seconds into shrouds.
For the trucks carrying
the appliances of death and devastation,
for the eager rescuer in his armoured car,
for the first visitor to the fabled homeland,
the graves of youths who died in confusion

are the only milestones to the city.
But the hills lie laced in mist.
Instead of your musk
I inhale the acrid smoke
of gelignite and pyres.

With cargoes of sand and mortar
Mammon came to inspect the city.
He cut down the remaining trees
and carried them away
like cadavers for dissection.
Morning papers like watered-down milk
hawk the same bland items:
rape, extortion, ambushes, confessions,
embezzlement, vendetta, sales, disappearances,
marriages, obituaries, the usual.

There is talk on the streets,
in dark corners, in homes, words
caught by the ears of a restaurant.
We honour the unvarying certainty,
and pay routine homage to silence.
Everyone has correctly identified
the enemy of the people.
He wears a new face each morning,
and freedom is asking yourself
if you are free, day after sullen day.

III

Uprightness is not caressing anything publicly,
Integrity is not drinking,
Worthiness is contributing generously to a new faith
to buy guns for unleashing ideological horror,
Service is milking the state
and when you can lift no more
to start burgling each other
so that we can become paragons of thievery,
Chastity is forbidding our women
from exposing their legs,
Purity is not whispering
even a solitary word of love
so that it will not be mistaken
for unpardonable obscenity.

Nothing is certain:
oil
lentils
potatoes
food for babies
transport
the outside world.
Even
fire water and air
are bought and sold.

Patriotism is the need of the season.
Patriotism is preaching secession
and mourning our merger with a nation,

patriotism is honouring martyrs
who died in confusion,
patriotism is declaring we should
preserve native customs, traditions,
our literature and performing arts,
and inflicting them on hapless peoples,
patriotism is admiring
the youth who fondles grenades,
patriotism is proclaiming all men as brothers
and secretly depriving my brother,
patriotism is playing the music of guns
to the child in the womb.

Stones and hills speak
when we finally run out of words.
History, hunch-backed friend,
why do we fear you?
Why do we love, hate, lie,
conceal, merely to enact you
in the coarse theatre of time?

IV

Today, I stand alone and acknowledge
the left-handed gift of a man
without a woman, and
a tiny land bound by fire.
Slave to an unexamined life
all that I've done
I've accomplished blindfolded:
love, fear, anger, and old despair.

The penitent year wears sackcloth
and pours ashen leaves on its head,
the sky's dress is in shreds.
When stars appear, they hold up the sky
like nuts and bolts so that
the firmament will not fall.
But we who sleep under these stars
will not let each other sleep.
Love is also a forgotten word.
The ability to suffer, and the power
to inflict harm
on what it loves most,
this is how I've known love.
The festival of lights
happened during childhood.
Today, I'm again with the widows
who cannot light lamps anymore.

Maybe the land is tired
of being suckled on blood,
maybe there is no peace
between the farmer and his fields,
maybe all men are tired of being men,
maybe we have acknowledged death.
My love, how can I explain
that I abhor laws
which punish a man for his past,
only the night seems to understand
that we must bear it again.

When I am gone
I would leave you these:
a life without mirrors, and
the blue ode between pines
and the winter sky.

But where can one run from the homeland,
where can I flee from your love?
They have become pursuing prisons
which hold the man
with criminal words.

Poem for Joseph

It is never too late to come home.
But I must first find a homeland
where I can find myself,
just a map or even a tree or a stone
to mark a spot I could return to
like an animal lifting his leg
even when there's nothing to return for.

Although it's true
that in my native land
children had crawled out of burrows
they had gouged under their hard beds,
long after the grownups had fled
and roofs came apart
like charred heads.

You said you didn't regret
how ethnic cleansers had palmed
your newly-built home off on a people
well on their trail back to unique blood,
you didn't mind leaving behind
objects of desire
you had collected over twenty-five years,
or, how you came to live in a rented room
with your wife and children
in dog-eat-dog Imphal,
among the callous tribe
I call my own.

Only the photographs you mourned,
the beloved sepia of a family tree,
since you're the reason why your fathers lived;
but who'll believe now
that you lived at all?

After 'Jashn-e-Azadi'

(a film on Kashmir by Sanjay Kak)

The kite transforming into smoke lacing
the chinars is not a symbol.
The rose has migrated from the garden of paradise.
Freedom will never come
poured into goblets waiting to be raised,
Martyrdom is a handout from the hagiographer.
Only poetry of ruins is real.
The incoherent rose still blooms
from some beloved breast torn open.

The First Rain

The first rain like the first letter of May
brings news to the hills.
Perched like the houses on the edge of a cliff
I've lived more days in exile
than years of my poor childhood.
As a fumbling fifteen-year-old
I abandoned my forward-looking native people
who entrusted terror, drugs and
a civilized plague to children.

Is it better to rejoice and forget
or to remember and be sad?
Only a foolish boy cannot wait to be a man,
adores winter, and leaves home to write poetry.

After the holocaust became a touchstone
we can indict an erring people
and make culture and carnage co-exist.
If I told you how babies have been shot down
from their mothers' breasts
you would put it down to a poet's overworked heart
but we like to believe in leaders who flock to the capital
only to fly back with spells as latter-day sorcerers.

An animal threatened with extinction
needs a lair for his mate and his young,
I'm not different.
I need the morning for its bright blood
and I need to seize the night.

There was not a day that changed my days.
When I listen to hills
I hear the voices of my faded life.
Whisky and Mehdi Hassan and Billie Holiday
make for strange fruit on nondescript evenings.

They can stop us but not our thoughts
from coming out into the streets,
they can shoot us but cannot kill the air
which carries our voices.

O my love, you are still asleep
when the rain carries the night till dawn.
After lying down with dreams of you
I awake in another day of bread and newspapers.

I'm banished to the last outpost of a dying empire
whose keepsakes have become the artefacts of the natives:
necklaces, pianos, lace and tombstones.
I've pursued horoscopes and
only promises and maledictions pursue me.
One day Venus was mine, joy and honey,
another day Saturn would not be propitiated.
I found a moment's peace
in my little daughter's face.

Before I met you
my dreams were limited by ignorance.
Sometimes at night
I put two drops of our past in my eyes
but they refused to close.

Can poetry be smuggled like guns or drugs?
We've drawn our borders with blood.
Even to write in our mother tongue
we cut open veins and our tongues
lick parchments with blood.

I read my smuggled Neruda
and sometimes listen to the fading fiddles
and the mourning voices of my land.

I'm the anguish of slashed roots,
the fear of the homeless,
and the desperation of former kisses.
How much land does my enemy need?

O my love, why did you fade
into the obscurity of my life
and leave me to look long at the mountain?

I'm the pain of slashed roots
and the last rain is already here.
I'll leave the cracked fields of my land
and its weeping pastures of daybreak.
Let wolves tear our beloved hills.

I'll leave the bamboo flowering
in the groves of my childhood.
Let rats gnaw at the supine map
of what was once my native land.

Native Land

First came the scream of the dying
in a bad dream, then the radio report,
and a newspaper: six shot dead, twenty-five
houses razed, sixteen beheaded with hands tied
behind their backs inside a church...
As the days crumbled, and the victors
and their victims grew in number,
I hardened inside my thickening hide,
until I lost my tenuous humanity.

I ceased thinking
of abandoned children inside blazing huts
still waiting for their parents.
If they remembered their grandmother's tales
of many winter hearths at the hour
of sleeping death, I didn't want to know,
if they ever learnt the magic of letters.
And the women heavy with seed,
their soft bodies mowed down
like grain stalk during their lyric harvests;
if they wore wildflowers in their hair
while they waited for their men,
I didn't care anymore.

I burnt my truth with them,
and buried uneasy manhood with them.
I did mutter, on some far-off day:
'There are limits,' but when the days
absolved the butchers, I continue to live
as if nothing happened.

The Dead

We must be dead.
Returning home at night
where love does not wait for us,
wolfing it down and breathing is not life.

During day we walk disembodied
as leaden ghosts in the streets.
Pressing our faceless features against windows
we see men and women drinking
and words form in our abyssal throats
but we cannot speak.
But those who ride away
leaving wisps of laughter behind
must be the living, the young man
and woman kissing in a corner
must be alive, although the grey-haired
man fetching withered greens
has already become one of us.
But those who dance and sing
must be naturally alive, even as
the terrorist who must stay alive
like the doctor who keeps death waiting
to prepare his rambling bill, so also
the traitor who must remain alive
to betray his comrades, and the prisoner
because he has an appointment with freedom.

The preacher is also alive—hellfire
and brimstone do their work, and
the terminal patient is alive because
of his wrenching pain. Only we are beyond pain,
and we refuse false resurrections.

Day after day we merely witness
scenes from the living, and
day by day we go on dying.
How long do the dead remain dead?
Even clothes come alive when they shelter bodies,
and the wind is alive if it can heave trees, and
the river because it can scar the stone's face.
The women we loved left us because
we died in their arms, we have no homeland,
no forwarding address, we must be dead.

We are sepulchral pages that preserve
the mortal remains of dreams, and awakened
at night when the living close their eyes
we cannot sleep. From our buried bodies
parasitic flowers have begun to bloom.
Once the living body was a flower too.

Middle-class Blues

A middle-class man
wakes up on a middle-class morning
and has his middle-class tea and biscuits.
Last night, he dreamt of being an aristocrat
but today he is afraid
of falling below the poverty line.
The middle class never begets rebels;
no one's rich enough to feel guilty about the poor
or poor enough to reach that breaking point.
A middle-class man merely wants to save his money
troubling no one and expecting no trouble in return.
Though he fell in love during his preindustrial youth
he eventually married a middle-class bride
and dutifully buys his middle-class fish,
constantly checking his middle-class watch.
On occasion, he may wear his single suit
but you can tell him
by his body odour and his shoes
although he may drive his middle-class car
and build his middle-class house
after scrimping and saving
all his lowbrow working life.

And although the irony will be lost on him
it's his money that keeps a democracy well oiled
because he pays his war taxes and earthquake dues
without a murmur of dissent.
And as grandfather grimbeard
who was buried in an English churchyard said,
many hold him in contempt
for his petty bourgeois ways.
Ah, it's as well that the petty bourgeois
never became rich or noble
and were spared such delusion.

Everywhere I Go...

Everywhere I go
I carry my homeland with me.
I look for it in protest marches on the streets of the capital,
in dark-maned girls of beauty contests
forced to waiting now behind windows.
I harbour the wretchedness of those youths
who do not wish to return
but would rather serve in a city's sordid restaurants
because devils and thieves rule their home.

I often hear about its future
in conflict resolution symposiums
where professors and retired generals
analyze the fate of my people and their misery.

But I can see it returning with women
and water in rural evenings.
And I want to tell my poet-friends
of the twelve mothers who stripped themselves
and asked soldiers to rape them.
In fact, I make imaginary journeys
to its little world every day
and wait for the fog of justice to lift
for a murdered eight-year-old girl.

Those who speak the language of progress
call my homeland a mendicant state
not knowing its landlocked misery,
its odd splendour.
And no one knows who picks up its bodies.

I know I must stop agonizing
(Perhaps I am the only one who broods about his land)
Even if people say
suffering must reach new heights
for a new beginning.
But whenever I touch my homeland's streets
everyone seems happy and has no grouses.
I must stop agonizing or save what I can
Such as the tunes of my homeland
which dance in my blood.

Last Word

What kind of a poet is he? they ask.
I said: 'I am a poet of earth and space,
possibly water, but not fire. I know
my limitations, and there are many things
between earth and sky I cannot name.
I have an ancient desire for understanding,
meaninglessness frightens me.
That is why I love simple things
such as sunlight on our shoulders,
or women with firm breasts
and hills quiet in the rain.'
They whispered among themselves:
'How come his poetry is riddled with bullets then?'
So I said:
'I wanted my poems to exude a heady odour
but only the sweet taint of blood
or burning flesh emanates from my poem.'
Then they said:
'His poems are always falling from arrogant heights.'
I answered:
'I've always wanted to see them fall
like leaves which turn beautiful before they die.'

But they said:
'When they fall his poems would shatter
because he drops them on stony ground.'
I only said:
'I wanted them to fall like pebbles
into a pool. I'm sorry I always break
my words on hostile surfaces.'
Finally they said:
'That is why his poetry is guarded.
He courts death and freedom but his words
need protection by an armed escort.
He could not speak and allowed
muteness to bind his heart.
This is the origin of his fear.'

NEW POEMS

15 August 2008, Northeast India

Having lost it
how could I celebrate my independence
though I've sewn flags on cockeyed schooldays?
Margins are superfluous in the big centre's book
although memory is not silent and speaks up at times.

Now the periphery (of which I'm also a smudged part)
is scrawling a unique history on delusive margins,
mischievous like a collage by brawling painters.
Once lebensraum has sunk to pogroms
the periphery can murder too
and then deal peace cards on the table
or hoist a nation's flag in driving rain.
On the continuum of farce
it doesn't matter if we're moving forward or backward
or if a government is serving rats on its menu.
The morning passes with a prime minister orating
from the ramparts of a fort,
'Make the borders irrelevant,' he said a year ago.
It never occurred to him to disguise himself and ask
the man on the street about his unhappiness.

On the road outside shut down by rebels
aimless now in its bafflement
trees and lamps are breathing fog and a light rain.
This day passes between surfing for news of the outside world,
statistics of farmers committing suicide on the weaver belt
and the poor waiting for paper to translate into bread

after discovering that a law has been enacted for them
which finds all of them culpable for shaming the nation.
And fifty years of discrimination festering in the periphery
with another anniversary of murder and disappearances.

I've been told that I live on the edge
by intellectuals who also teach me
the history and politics of faraway countries.
I have to take their word on faith, being so unread.
I don't know if I'm shallow, with little inner life.
I try not to book a flat in the city of the sky
but meditate brokenly on love and its gamblers
although she gave me a terrible fright the other day.
I merely silenced her shame with my mouth
and remain a freeloader of passion from its web.

Father on Earth

With a shambling gait
my father whips out his dick
and pisses like a dog.
He's eighty-six and lost his reason.
Not quite, for when he loses his temper
he blurts out: 'Dog's cunt.'
But the man who never prayed
when I was a kid
and asked us to burn his horoscope
is now humming hymns.
What is the matter with him?
Is it the strain of dementia
which is supposed to run in the family?
Is he penitent about his infidelities?

I remember his gentle physician's hands
that mended my fractured fears
as a child,
his joke about village dogs
refusing to bark at Rip Van Winkle,
his histrionic tale of Bremen's musicians.

My mother, long-suffering and prejudiced,
can never catch a wink when he shouts
in the dead of night as his demons needle him.
But she often holds his hands and caresses them
and talks to him as one would to a child.
She's been doing this for years now.
So it must be love.
My father now mimics my little daughter.
In fact, he is the son I never fathered.

Body

Because I couldn't examine it from close quarters
like Burton with his magnifying glass
I worshipped it from afar.
The body is never free of the human condition
and either weeps or sings, or becomes restive
if denied bacchanalia or tragedy.
Time is not its enemy as Ovid would have it
but the mind with its dark pledges.
If you kick a body as Descartes demonstrated
it reacts violently, for it isn't the soul which replies
but flesh and bone with their
entire moral and philosophical apparatuses.
The body is the key to Adam's children,
heathen matter that mystics want to defeat.
Serial killers want to destroy it
as it often turns up in court as witness,
rapists in uniform want to reduce it to pulp
because it conceals intimate evidence,
poets want to disembody it to elegize fallen man.
But the body is the sum of its parts.
Sever an organ and the tongue takes over,
remove a hand and the foot starts painting,
deny eyes and fingers are already on the keys.

Marriages and Funerals

I've stopped going to marriages and funerals. Any demonstration of grief or joy unnerves me. Solemnity withers me and dark sartorial elegance moves no one. It's not that I've forgotten kindness or to wish people happiness if they can find it. I could help the bereaved furtively after the mourners have eaten and left. I have become truly unsociable.

I can't fathom why anyone would like to be comforted except by people they love selfishly. You only need hugs and kisses from people who give you, when pressed, your morsel of flesh. I cannot be comforted, except by the woman I love illicitly.

I often wonder about the efficacy of marriages and funerals. Could it be because others are as worried as I was during my own wedding feast that my friends would not show up for some mystifying reason? As regards funerals, I know that if the house of the dead cannot keep a demonic hold on me my absence will not make any difference. But I don't want to be censured for not attending marriages or funerals. I wish people would not invite me to weddings or bring news of an old acquaintance's death. If I could I wouldn't attend even my own funeral.

I remember the day I returned home, and without even seeing my father I went to my aunt's house when I heard my cousin had died during my long absence. I tried to match my aunt's grief by showing some stubborn tears in my eyes but ended up sniffing like a dog. After that, my cousin's sister, my other lovely cousin, in whose body I first sang a liquid tune, gave me pineapple to eat and we smiled at each other. I used to dip my hands into her blooming breasts, a pair of frightened pigeons. But later, my dead cousin appeared in my dreams to play and protect me again as he did during our childhood. He took a long time to go away and I had to spit three times to make sure that he wouldn't haunt me.

I remember this film about slum-dwellers in Bombay and how after the tears and the burning they would bring out their bottles of orange liquor and get drunk and have a real ball. That's one funeral I would like to attend.

My Invented Land

(after Mario Meléndez)

My native soil was created from tiny sparks
that clung to grandmother's earthen pot
which conjured savoury dishes
I've been looking for
all my life in vain.

My homeland has no boundaries.
At cockcrow one day it found itself
inside a country to its west,
(on rainy days it dreams looking east
when its seditionists fight to liberate it from truth.)

My people have disinterred their alphabet,
burnt down decrepit libraries
in a last puff of nationalism,
even as a hairstyle of native women
has been allowed to become extinct.

My native place has not been christened yet
my homeland, a travelogue without end,
a plate that will always be greedy
(but got rice mixed with stones.)

My home has young people
who found their dreams in a white substance
and the old that transplanted their eyes,
it has leaders who have disappeared
into their caricatures.

My home is a gun
pressed against both temples
a knock on a night that has not ended
a torch lit long after the theft
a sonnet about body counts
undoubtedly raped
definitely abandoned
in a tryst with destiny.

Saint Edmund's College

(after Jotamario Arbeláez)

To Basu, gardener, who marijuana kept alive
To an Irish Brother, shipwrecked in a hill-station
Facta Non Verba

Grafted at fifteen
on Lum Mawrie hill
one winter I kindled
pine needles, cones, branches
on its burnt sienna slope,
avoiding fetes,
fiercely intelligent classmates,
but lusting after the nymphs
who came to smoke in the forest,
or watching movies
in the school hall
while the principal smirked
at demurely horrified Loreto Convent girls
during a naked scene.

I avoided the principal's
German shepherds
lurked in the corridors
severed nude Greek goddesses
inside the library of gravitas,
took my turn at graffiti
on the toilet wall.
The future is in your hands

shake well after use,
if you shake it more than once
you're playing with it,
they said.

At economics class
Adam Smith, the father himself,
hawked and spat
and asked me if I didn't sleep the night before
while the brother who taught chemistry
advised a classmate to take a formula on faith
when he failed to grasp it.
The geography teacher
during his frothy lecture on African rivers asked
why my friend laughed like a crocodile.

On many fluid days
I inhabited parallel worlds
of tailors and boarding houses
of barbers and books
of hostel and bar,
speculated on sex and movies
with little money in my pocket,
and only one pair of shoes
but many roads.

Postcard

(for Nigel)

To bear the fate
of the crossing alone,
drink bitter brew by yourself in ports.
Only the bravado that comes
to put off a savage loneliness.

Will the Ceredigion sun be as kind when
the archdruid lies under an *englyn* of leaves?

Remember the night that lay fastened to a ship's deck
when he and I returned after seeing Penelope.
Glasses purloined from a midnight café,
iridescent stars above the sea's boulevards,
winking until a dawn awash with unearthly shades.

I read his obituary again, contrite enough
to want to visit his grave, and come to listen
to Arthur's blood lapping your stones.

Salt

The kings of my country
would sometimes sacrifice a poor widow
who had only a little daughter in the world
when a salt spring couldn't be found.

When I find it crystallised around my eyelids
I would not remember
why they formed at all.

Postcard

(for Jayanta Mahapatra)

Over the years, woodwork
protest in all shades of weather,
a mango tree fell in a storm.
I occupy the old room in your house,
a poet, mellifluous, another quiet nook;
like the ones who once came uninvited,
passed away, or just left,
defenceless in their infidelity.

The rooms turned emptier in their pleas,
and no one looked down from your balcony.
Just a few flowering trees,
visiting lizards, chipmunks, in the midst
of a stone forest's marauding.
You said the trees thwart the swooping dust
and bring birds.

Nights grow shriller now,
ghosts leaving friends on the road,
shades who spoke when spoken to,
as a little girl near Trang Bang
flees across your writing table
dumb in her screaming.

Spring's Torment

I

Tonight on, we'll speak without speaking,
the unearthed etymology of jealousies now shut.
Diminished like the world, we
feel what orphans, lowlifes, trees, dogs feel.

Why do we return to a room
where nights beat the day sadly?
Why did derelict clocks stop at midnight,
and photographs begin wearing dusty jackets?

Neither ghost nor living,
something under the cover of the hills' night
goes to your street in quest of lips.

II

I should have sucked you in me,
I am lost without your fingers,
your healing oils,
my terrestrial hours inhaled without
a thought for the world

But looking under sheets
of twilight, for the left anklet
you lost, for me to search each time
and claim its owner.

I long to hear you moan again
in your native tongue,
scribbled across my night's skin.

With birds whooping spring across treetops
green days taken away from us
will be divided among blue lovers.

III

Your smile conceives another dawn
when stars tousled your downcast hair.
I recovered from your lips what I knew to be
constant as midnight water
in the thirsty glass.

When I put my mouth on yours
I turn blind and deaf, the earth must wait.
Even as we speak, we become wet
with early dew.

The world returned
with all its intrigues,
its streets and smoke as our lips separate,
with schools of hatred, and renewed
hunger for bread.

IV

If only you would walk like spring
before my window's heart, before
the blinding rain which drowned
your ankles and keep us divided
between bent latitudes.

The sky is a slow throbbing lead today,
a juvenile fluttering of watery wings
begin on my foreboding panes, the chandeliers
of pine sway drunk, casting away their yellow radiance,
fires which sprout green bring doused
only the faint cinder of hours remains.

And the day's torrent takes you away
in a submerged bus with broken windows
running carefully with my memories.

September

I'm a brown dervish leaf on a forgotten cobweb.
All voyages will be inward from now,
a late train pulling away from a station and
no hand waves in answer outside its grimy window
to say: 'I meant everything I said.'
When it arrives with a yellow accusation of leaves
there will be days enough to rue
many wordless days with her.

Violated by rain, air and birds
cherries begin to rustle sadly above the earth.
But when the cold cuts
they will fan out like fallen women.

If only we could return our blood
to the leaves, the end would be bearable.
Now fall, long-awaited wine,
burns in our veins.
Flash of sunlight brushing rough bark,
naive month saying goodbye
in the midst of foliate dreams.

October

We are waiting inside houses
of cloud-catching mountains
for the resolute flutes of rain to stop.
Herded all along the highway in slime
a last wave of leaves, displaced by a regime,
through perforated awnings of October trees
jostle to cross a wide transmigratory river,
remembrance-laden leaf-boats.

Something made us lonelier
we let too many immigrants into our hearts,
disproportionate future left us speechless.

Understanding

I can understand on this virtual day
even without smelling,
let alone touching it. So,
I'll not say a word
about the sea giving up a toddler.
I can even understand
this groundswell of feeling
as if humanity were testing its waters,
after adapting a short brackish tragedy,
despite pleas from the gentlest mourner not to use
the image of drowning
but only remember a child's smile,
in an age whose only metaphysical worry is,
'what can be saved?',
trees, animals, or children, for instance,
late after the mocking, 'ecstatic destruction'.

Spring

Trees fated to lie down
whisper in the wind among pines that
they want to resurrect in the forest's spell.
Unbidden, peach blossoms of torment
fan out under silken clouds.

Smoking boys with catapults come to kill birds and
the plum, gnarled by winter, shouts at them
to leave, because he is deadened
without birds hopping from his arms, the
squirrels scampering on his craggy shin.
But the plum puts out immaculate flowers
for a single hailstorm to ruin them fruitless.

At night, under the yellow pollen of remembrance
the tree being desire-racked cannot sleep and
wakes with rheumy eyes at dawn.

January

A stranded train of hurt and memory offloads us at winter's coming.
Something freezes birdsong and
we see only ashen arms of woodless trees. And
even if you hum with cold, January will not leave.
Will the bluebird ever return to the heart's forked branches?
I imagine a world bereft of snow, and
waiting for the sixth extinction
watch giant fish beached by plastic.
The time is here for you to forgive me
for wounding the sleeping furry animal of your thighs.
On that road stretched taut between us
only a mist and granite sadness has remained.
If anyone were so much as to mention a word like 'love'
everything will fall quietly again as snow.

Learner

A pup out on the road the very first time
high on adrenaline and psychotropic substances.
My little daughter only said
remember the left pedal's the clutch
the middle one the brakes.
After you've found your hands and legs and head
could do a little jig together
always let old women and the cows cross first,
don't let the boys riding on a two-legged Thanatos or
taxi drivers blasting away heavy rock while abusing lanes
drive you into murderous rage, and above all,
expect the unexpected
like the nutcrackers materialising without
any white warning on a road you think is buttery.
The road was not built by your father.

Flight

The warning disguised as a message
came before the village was up and about,
and when they left
they didn't carry pots or blankets
or even machetes.
As they went to the outpost of guardians
they left chickens running in the yard
and the dog lazing on the steps.

Flights like theirs
do not have destinations,
and only once did they wish for wings.

The taste of the herd will return them
to dark and dingy towns where
they can sell used clothes, wild meat and herbs.
The most vulnerable will sell bodies.
Because in spite of the landmines
they still shared limbs.

Words like 'the end of history'
will not resonate anywhere in their lives.
They do not have meat and drinks left
to offer to embedded scribes
as newspapers have died on them. Like before
their fates will go unreported, arousing
only a lukewarm curiosity somewhere.

Forgetting

When we become forgetful
we cannot remember what gives us pause
on days which seem to never end.
To forget is to die once more
through Moses's Egypt to the Wuhan spectacle.
Creatures, animate or not
still journey on bravely, slighting borders,
coal, dazed refugees, torpedoes, mountain goats,
even as pestilence brokers have begun roaring:
'The economy is dead!
Long live the economy!'
We notice streets bereft of children,
luxury yachts for the first time while
a goods train leisurely flattens
a curve of migrant workers
and snow-crowned peaks
swim into view daily on grimy streets.
We cannot mask an ineffable fear
unlike emperor penguins marching
in a dignified line toward extinction.

Winter Chronicle

(after Neruda)

If you were to put a new heart in me
with your meagre lips, on the cold face
of these walls a blue day will break
on the brooding hills, a dead wind
will rise with spring and a banished sun
will be recalled from exile, if you would
give me a new heart at the cruel end of my day.

There are unfinished things burning
in desire without love, these are eyes
which gazed into hell's mouth and returned
blinded. On every corner of earth man sets up
his governments and inadequate laws, his
boundaries between hearts and territories,
his cunning shops with which he hopes to dominate,
so here begins the city of the fortune-hunters.
When man devised means to leave himself alone
he exists like a beast, eating, defecating, his
dreams growing wild with his reasoning, his
loneliness added in cold figures in narrow
dingy rooms, and converted into a learned beast
he merely roams in a civilized jungle.
What happens to immaculate voices embalmed in pages
of clammy rooms, what happens to learning
and purists in streets and on pavements?

My love, I've only inherited his foolish legacy
even before we existed. Now I tell you
the other truth of the same river which
gives us voices and wets our eyes, I disclose
the nakedness of our skin from leaves and feathers,
I bare the latent music in our souls
from birds and the sea. I am talking of the love
we borrowed from animals, but not the sorrow
we weave from our human bonds. When I tire
of man's feats, his proud trophies, his
patent discoveries and inventions, I return to
the blunt end of desire, and like any solitary man
who always searches when nothing comes his way I live
in dread of strange timepieces, vanquished by the day
and quarantined by night. My love, an unknown presence
lurks everywhere, and neither prayer nor logic can drive
the names away.

So we return as rice and wine to earth
but think of me as your day and your night,
not the day which begins with the clock's axiom,
with traders and soldiers united by a collective desire,
and merchandise carefully pressed and laid out like clothes,
with guns cleaned and oiled, ensured of smooth functioning,
and butchers washing dried blood from their blocks into
small rivers, with grocers renovating early vegetables.
Restive as ants, everywhere man wants to plant his flag,
for his phallic colossi sprouting arrogantly from the bowels
of earth, stony without passion, he even maims
his own memorials. Having emerged from his prehistoric
cave, he surpassed his feral brethren, and perfected

savagery by splitting the atom, by raining obscene death
from the skies, death which clings to the flesh of
children in faceless hamlets. Bound to brutal history
which refines lying, man defers his lessons, and
one hand never washes the other. So we continue
with the hours beginning with torture and ending
with rape, and after the dissolution of regimes
he meticulously exhumes his crimes with mass graves
punishing the killers he has nourished, and rewarding
the already-senile heroes. But he turns his eyes
away from starving children, and wants
to speak to intelligent beings by bridging
interstellar gorges. So how far has man walked from
his cave when during his waking hours he is trapped inside
his buildings, in his own cages with mice, playing God
with viruses and particles, inhaling the
fetid breath of machines, and even his young are not spared
when they are made to perform like circus animals before
sadistic adults? But civilization throws ashes in his eyes,
covering him in foppery, persuading him 'to cultivate the opera
in evenings and sip vintage, to hang masterpieces on walls', and
dissect learned books, gentling his tongue until death sends his
emissary, soliciting man's presence, and the animals draw near,
baring guns and grenades, and they wouldn't even reveal
which century we are living in.

My love, night flings its dark shroud across the hills
but we have already paid the price to the boatman.
We know death but our lives are dear, although the grim
ravenpriests of time are wheeling above us. And in the
mountains with their great rains your name grew out of earth,

burning again in the heart of time. So I shall survive this
storm of leaves and words, I shall salvage the wreck of sunken
youth by yielding to retrieve broken things, if the rain also
stitches the fissures of earth. And I seek growth and moisture,
not the dark weight of a stone, unwilling to grow old with a
censorious tongue, seedless, resigned to death,
petrifying by degrees.

My love, even the darkness is broken by howls
and dripping water, the clock again awaits dawn,
but when I uncovered the word in my hand
it spelt loneliness. My love, night conspires with
the wind whispering black secrets once more.
If only you would give me your hand, a day
dressed in blue will dance on these cold walls
consuming my winter-to-winter sadness.

Poet

Why do trees weep leaves without warning?
Why do the old choose to die in their mountain hamlets?
Why did his people turn to terror?
Why does love tie him down?
How is he a poet if he doesn't know how to ask for answers?

The Garden

The one who arrives late
must pay the price of finding
a city in ruins with a garden in its heart.
Wonder, fear, and regret
accompany such an arrival like
the one who falls in love but meets
the beloved late, bearing a stone's weight
on the circumspect heart, despite
the hypnotic attraction of ruins.
He will embrace her who strangers have,
drink from lips others have kissed.

The others have been here
when the city was being built,
partaking in its revelries,
only to abandon the destroyed city
so that they can soar as archangels
in search of young, voluptuous cities.
But he will paint wretched pictures
of boats moored to silence, and
when he asks his guide of ruins,
'Who lived in this house, this city?'
He will get the reply, 'Love.'

'Every leaf, every shrub in the garden
Knows his heart's condition,'
do not step into that garden
seeking forgiveness for the first sin.

At Noh Ka Likai's

Mist in your heart you stood
above the fall at land's lip,
cold thinned
by a water-coloured day.
The dwellings seemed lonely far below,
a silence shrieked from vale to vale.

Once very old gods came to play
in those hellish gorges, complete
with white beards and thundering laughter,
once before the sad young god came
to cloister your soul. But we went
to only say goodbye for summer there.

At the horizon
rivers of another country shimmered,
changed by distance into myth,
their faces veiled
by the fine braiding of the rain.
We only had to drink the silver waters
before the random return of legends:
in a woman lured from her cave by flowers,
a serpent of ages who had lived on
with mere human blood.

When winds severed a cord, unmooring boats,
we watched variations of green
on plums flanking our crossing paths,
stumbling upon the disappeared that eluded us
back in the midst of a forest of stone.
Wondering how others have
learnt their living, you magically
softened all too briefly beside me
with fog and drizzle in your hair.

Speaking

My neighbourhood's erstwhile Marxist and comrade
with whom I grew taller together
who once worshipped farmers, workers, peasants,
after turning a motherland-worshipping politician
genuinely concerned about the endangered species
of our race and mother tongue
admonished me recently, 'Writing poems is fine
but think of doing a bit for your homeland.'
An ageing poet-brother blurted out one day,
'My poems you translated yourself
are lying abandoned under your bed.
Do try to make them see that light of day.
What if I were to croak suddenly?'
My long-suffering wife too
said about an off-and-on callous daughter,
'Don't know about others, but being my child
I can't help caring about her.'
Weighed down with misdeeds
I know I long forfeited my right to speak but
haven't stopped speaking to ants and birds.
Just the other day, a falling tree
with her dying breath told me
about her wrenching pain, and I
could understand her perfectly.

Home

Slippery patch between head and heart
that home for the aged.

A brother who held his hand to the hilltop
where a shrine to the benign goddess stood
until his brother let go of his hand,
a sister who sang 60s pop when dancing
the twist across his marvelling eyes
until her mind twisted with forgetting,
a river that raged and hypnotised him,
like a small prey, with swirling brown waters
until it died, strangled by garbage,
a wasp-nesting attic where he pored
over stolen adult books until the attic
flew away one night with his fantasies,
a pillow inside which he hid
his first letter of love,
a star's droppings.

Silence

Silence
no longer seemed
anything like a melody.
For Michelangelo
crickets chirping in his ears
became strident
with the birth of night.
Did the thought
of the Sistine ceiling
lull him to sleep at last?
In the cold nights
awaiting a masterpiece
a longing grows
for a human voice,
spotted doves,
a dripping tap,
fading horns,
the frequency of rain
he lost in marbled Carrara.

Speculation on Spring

Even when spring's here, it's cold inside my sunless room where I've been sitting for fifteen years. Everything—books, clothes, appliances—is coated in a layer of powder and grit. March had brought pine pollen, its wayward winds more ashes, and this old house with its decaying walls and roof even more dust. I think I could have changed my fate just a fraction. But for many years I didn't want to—call me timid or unmotivated. You can change your fate just by meeting people who matter but you don't want to meet someone who may be unfriendly and unhelpful. I step out of this room only when there's a hint of sunlight outside. I see girls wearing summer tees while I wear a jacket with my neck covered. The girls remind me of the plumber who struts about with a short-sleeved cotton shirt in the depth of winter, sometimes with a *bidi* between his fingers. I call him 'Mr Winter Challenger'. If I head towards the cherry trees which blossomed brazenly during each November, I'll see small luminous blood-red berries on the ground, crunched or half-eaten. This is a wild cherry, its fruit has an acidic taste and I don't know if it's poisonous. No wonder the birds only pecked at them. In nature, birds, animals, trees, flowers have their twins like double entendres. There's a small hibiscus—red like its bigger cousin, but elongated in shape and used as an offering during prayers to household deities. Cherries too have their counterparts, the small inedible ones with riotous pink blossoms, and the edible ones which come to the market from far away. I remember my Welsh poet-brother, who packed for me a lunch box of dark delicious cherries when I left his house in Swansea to catch a train when dawn was breaking. That was the last time I saw him. His grave lies seas away, waters I can't cross anymore.

Only the other day, the pestilence came very near, within breathing distance. I had been filled with fear again for many days. I know I must start writing again as if inside a confessional, and must then tear up the guilt and anxieties I recorded in a breathless hurry.

Day

I walk in a backyard
in fear of a street's air
within an instant's perimeter,
no longer in conversation
with blue birds or camouflaged moths
but only a prisoner allowed a little sun
during a prolonged sentence,
praying each dawn
for the mindless numbers to drop
so that a primeval need
may be restored to us:
the ability to hold another
before the day ends.

Birds

They have every instinct
to be wary, of men.
I have every reason to watch them
hopping, chirpy in twos or threes
feathers unruffled now, gaining air and
the ground's confidence
during a man-wrought pestilence.
More than a year
of staring at them and
I've learnt nothing
of their language.

A Street, Vellore

As little shrines toll their bells
I navigate through cowpats on mornings when
schoolgirls with swinging ponytails cannot know
where their bodies will lie on their fateful day.
A random bullock cart grapples with omnipresent bikes and muscular cars.
A woman who serves coffee with a shower cap on
smiles comfortingly, oblivious of the hobbling waiter
who hasn't changed but knows I drink mine without sugar.
A cursing one slashes a lane with blocks of ice as
a young boy walks on it but in a wheelchair,
the garbage pits pinch your nose
in the winging heat as flies land unerringly on your lip.
Another boy has a hand floating in a cylinder with spokes when
a man sells divinities with only stumps as gifts from leprosy.
But there are buxom women, darkly beautiful
with flowers in their buns scattering a heady scent.
It has churches surrounded by temples that climb
right up to a steep hill, its nude boulders blazing in the sun
with a faraway faith.
At where I thought this street slowed
a lone mosque drowns all around with its azan.
And all its contents spilling onto it at unwary corners,
having burst life's seams are held together
by a hospital in the middle of it.
I felt sad for the young girl in quiet pain and
gave her mother a polythene bag because
the girl couldn't keep anything down, unknowing
that my own days would be at sea thereafter.

Disturbed by the women without hair, a high frequency
metallic voice from space returns me to earth—only an old man
calling a woman frantically in code.
I often lose all desire on this street
but only wish to see some faces before I quit this place
with a hospital for its heart.
If only one end leads to mountains or
the other to the sea, this street
cannot infect me with the curiosity
of what lies at its end or beginning.
If it's an indifferent continuum, I must be in medias res.

Autumn

No more telltale signs of the war's touch
on these forests of October,
the gouged earth manicured into gardens.

I'm thinking the rescue of your hands,
the brown leaf of your eyes
covering the wounded ground.

Elsewhere, abandoning bereft lovers
heroes are marching off
to history's drumbeats.

Mawlai

Day still ambles along in a neighbourhood
an adolescent was wary of stealing into,
unfamiliar hills with a wild reputation.
Dark green roof of pine grove, houses
with looked-after flowers, a pear tree each.
Across the road, from a meat stall
a boy chases away a cat lazily,
at a saw's hum a sleepy old man
leans on his veranda railing.
This is where I want to meet
an old love beautiful as a summer's day
to ask her how she has been.

Six Impure Haiku

Spring calling cuckoo—
warmly feeding snowy tears
a high mountain cheek.

June's yellow-green leaves
deceiving me with autumn,
ashes from Auschwitz.

In the woodpecker's quiet pause
I glimpse an afternoon in the pines.
Am I stepping into
the same season twice?

Rain drips away in the heart room.
Photo or book
which one to rescue?

November sky.
Wise, clear-eyed heart—
cold star fluttering in the pines.

Drab cherry blossoms,
hill winter's azure sky
the only remedy.

ACKNOWLEDGEMENTS

I am thankful to Ravi Singh of Speaking Tiger Books for reposing faith in my poetry by readily agreeing to publish this book and to Vineetha Mokkil, a discerning editor, who made valuable suggestions. I am deeply indebted to Anjum Hasan, well-known fictionist and poet, for her vital role in putting these poems together when I was unsure where they would moor. I am obliged to Tarun Bhartiya, filmmaker, photographer, Shillong-based activist and poet, for supporting this project and airing my verse. Many thanks to Tarun for the cover photograph titled 'Storm Before the Monsoon Rain 2017, Nellie, Assam'. My heartfelt appreciation goes to Dhruba Hazarika, a recognized fictionist, for his continued heartening in these poetically bleak times.

Grateful acknowledgment is due to the publishers of the following collections from which the selected poems were drawn:

Words and the Silence, Writers Workshop, 1988.

Time's Crossroads, Orient Longman Limited, 1994.

The Desire of Roots, Chandrabhaga, 2006 and Red River, 2019.

I am grateful to the editors of the following anthologies and magazines where versions of some of the poems and previously unpublished ones appeared: *New Statesman & Society*; *Planet: The Welsh Internationalist*; the *Literary Review*; *Verse*; *The New Welsh Review*; *Kunapipi*; *Poetry Wales*; *Kavya Bharati*; *Chandrabhaga*; *The Telegraph Colour Magazine*; *Debonair*; *Nether*; *Poiesis*; *Indian Literature*; *Khasia in Gwalia*; *Confronting Love: Poems*; *Where the Sun Rises When Shadows Fall: The North-east*; *These My Words: The Penguin Book of Indian Poetry*; *The HarperCollins Book of English*

Poetry; *Another Country: An Anthology of Post-Independence Indian Poetry in English; The Himalayan Arc; brown critique Home Anthology; Witness: The Red River Book of Poetry of Dissent; Future Library: Contemporary Indian Writing; The Penguin Book of Indian Poets.*

A version of my introductory essay first appeared in *Indian Literature* 227, Vol. XLIX, No.3, May-June 2005 (Sahitya Akademi, Delhi).